Bonsai
for
Beginners

The Art and Science
of Growing Miniature Trees

Luca Morales

TABLE OF CONTENTS

INTRODUCTION

Welcome to the world of bonsai

A long-revered art form known as bonsai attracts admirers with its miniature trees, which represent the harmony and beauty of nature. With a rich history and culture, bonsai has traveled over time and space to become a well-liked hobby and form of artistic expression on a global scale. We will go into the fascinating world of bonsai in this section, looking at its history, relevance, and the tremendous effects it has on those that take this journey.

Ancient China is where bonsai originated, and there, miniature tree cultivation dates back more than a thousand years. It used to be a sort of elite-only art that stood for riches and authority. The Chinese term penjing, which translates to "tray scenery," included the construction of miniature landscapes with figurines, pebbles, and trees. This custom slowly spread to Japan and developed into what is now known as bonsai.

Beyond simple horticulture or gardening, bonsai represents much more. It captures the deep bond between people and the natural environment. The meticulous care to detail and nurture necessary for bonsai development encourage patience and focus. Every tree has a unique narrative that captures the essence of the artist's vision as well as the passage of time. Bonsai inspires us to take a moment, think, and recognize the beauty that exists even in the most minute details.

At its foundation, bonsai is an artistic medium. To create living sculptures, it blends design, aesthetics, and workmanship principles. The purposeful styling and shape of trees, which imitates forms found in nature while incorporating the artist's original ideas, is where the creativity rests. Years of meticulous pruning, wiring, and training produce the beautiful, symmetrical compositions of bonsai trees that convey a sense of balance and calm. Each tree has an own personality that reflects the artist's talent and the message they want to portray.

The capacity of bonsai to bring nature indoors is one of its most alluring features. Many people turn to bonsai gardening as a way to escape the growing urbanization and re-establish their connection to nature. Even in the constraints of an apartment or office, bonsai offers the chance to see and appreciate the exquisite beauty of trees up close. People develop a strong connection with nature and a sense of responsibility and stewardship by tending to and caring for a bonsai tree.

The art of bonsai demands patience, commitment, and a great eye for detail. Careful observation and exact execution are necessary while shaping and training a bonsai tree. A bonsai tree can take decades to develop, so patience is a must. Practitioners of this art form learn the value of perseverance and the benefits of putting in time and effort. As they immerse themselves in the art and find satisfaction in the present moment and the gradual but steady growth of their trees, bonsai enthusiasts acquire a stronger feeling of mindfulness.

Working with bonsai may be really meditative. Practitioners might find inner peace and tranquility in the focused attention needed to wire, prune, and maintain bonsai trees. When working with their trees, bonsai enthusiasts frequently speak of a sense of calmness and peace since they are totally focused on what they are doing. This contemplative feature of bonsai not only enhances mental health but also enables people to develop a deeper awareness of themselves and their relationship to nature.

The art of bonsai is well embedded in the culture of Japan and other nations where it is popular. The finest examples of this art form are displayed in renowned exhibitions and contests in Japan, where bonsai is regarded as an essential part of their culture. Additionally, bonsai has grown in popularity in a number of Western countries, where it is valued for its elegance and as a representation of awe for the beauty of nature. Language barriers are irrelevant when it comes to bonsai since this ancient art unites individuals from all over the world in a common passion.

Welcome to the fascinating world of bonsai, where miniature trees transform into living manifestations of nature and art. People all over the world have fallen in love with bonsai due to its lengthy history, relevance, and artistic appeal. This style of art provides an opportunity to cultivate mindfulness, patience, and a closer relationship with nature in addition to beauty. May you experience delight, inspiration, and a renewed respect for nature's many beauties as you begin your journey into the world of bonsai.

Brief history and significance of bonsai

The practice of growing miniature trees, known as bonsai, has a long history that crosses many different eras and countries. Bonsai, which originated in China and was later adopted by Japan, has changed from being a revered form of artistic expression and a profound connection with nature to a symbol of wealth and power. We shall delve into the intriguing background of bonsai, its cultural relevance, and the enduring influence it was given on people and communities all around the world in this section.

The art of growing miniature trees has its origins in ancient China, where it has been practiced for more than a thousand years. Penjing, which translates to "tray scenery," was originally a Chinese art style that involves building miniature landscapes with figures, rocks, and trees. These meticulously produced images sought to condense the essence of natural surroundings into a small area. The representation of nature in penjing art extended beyond just depicting trees.

Trade and cultural interactions between China and Japan were thriving throughout the Tang Dynasty in China. The practice of penjing was brought to Japan at this period, where it over time evolved into what is now known as bonsai. The miniature trees' capacity to bring up the beauty and essence of nature in a small area captured the attention of Japanese artists and monks. Over time, bonsai developed a close bond with Japanese spirituality and culture.

With the influence of Zen Buddhism and Japanese aesthetics, bonsai in Japan developed a distinctive personality. The bonsai art incorporates the wabi-sabi aesthetic's emphasis on simplicity, imperfection, and the fleeting nature of things. The art of bonsai evolved to represent a peaceful union of the wild and the cultivated, representing the idea that there is beauty in simplicity and acceptance of life's flaws.

The samurai class in Japan began to become more and more interested in bonsai during the Kamakura period. Samurai warriors who were steeped in the Zen Buddhism traditions discovered comfort and inspiration in the art of bonsai. The meticulous attention to detail, discipline, and care needed to grow bonsai were characteristics of the samurai. In a world of conflict and chaos, bonsai became a way to cultivate inner tranquility and peace.

The elite in ancient Japan were the first to pursue bonsai. The ownership and preservation of bonsai trees were regarded as symbols of power, wealth, and social standing. Bonsai were frequently displayed in ornate gardens and palaces, and nobles and aristocrats would hire expert artists to make and take care of them. Bonsai evolved as a way to express one's social standing in addition to providing aesthetic enjoyment.

With time, bonsai transcended its connection to wealth and power and opened up to a larger range of people. It gained recognition as a distinctive kind of artistic expression. Trees can be shaped and styled using sophisticated techniques developed by bonsai artists that combine design, aesthetics, and craftsmanship. Each bonsai tree developed into a living sculpture, embodying the artist's ideas and resembling a full-sized tree in miniature.

Nature is held in high regard in Japanese culture. This respect is embodied in bonsai, which enables people to experience the beauty and tranquility of nature everyday. Growing bonsai is a method to get in touch with nature and foster a sense of balance and harmony. Since bonsai trees are thought of as living things, knowledge of their behavior and life cycle is necessary for their proper care. People who take care of bonsai have a deep respect for the subtle wonders of nature.

Japan opened its doors to the outside world in the 19th century, allowing Westerners to experience Japanese art and culture. Western artists and collectors were enthralled by bonsai's distinct beauty and meaning. After being introduced to the West, bonsai created a passion with this ancient art form, and enthusiasts began growing bonsai all over the world. Western artists began to be influenced by bonsai, which changed how they viewed nature and the bonsai art form.

Bonsai still has a significant place in the fast-paced, urbanized world of today. It serves as a reminder of how crucial it is to take our time, appreciate the beauty all around us, and find moments of quiet and peace despite the daily chaos. Growing bonsai gives people a sense of direction, connects them to the cycles of nature, and enables them express their creativity. In addition to creating a sense of community, bonsai encourages it by bringing people together who share a common interest in the art form.

In conclusion, the history of bonsai is proof of the significance and ongoing attraction of this age-old craft. From its beginnings in China to its significant impact on Japanese culture and subsequent global diffusion, bonsai has captivated the interests of people from all walks of life. Beyond only being aesthetically pleasing, bonsai represents a close relationship with nature, a reflection of cultural values, and a way to express oneself. Let's continue to cultivate this valued art form, preserving its traditions while accepting its expanding significance in contemporary society, as we acknowledge the long history of bonsai.

Benefits of growing bonsai

The practice of cultivating miniature trees, or bonsai, offers benefits beyond simply aesthetic appeal. It is a fun and rewarding hobby that offers many advantages to those who take the chance. Growing bonsai has several benefits for enthusiasts, from improving patience and mindfulness to cultivating a sense of connection with nature.

This section will examine the several advantages of bonsai cultivation and how it can significantly improve our quality of life.

It takes a lot of patience and attention to detail to grow bonsai. A bonsai tree must be trained and shaped over a long period of time, frequently years or even decades. As practitioners immerse themselves in the present and pay attention to the tiny modifications in their trees, this methodical approach fosters a sense of mindfulness. Bonsai enthusiasts acquire a greater understanding of the interconnection of all living things as well as the beauty of slow, gradual growth.

A connection to nature is something that many people seek for in today's hectic and urbanized society. Growing bonsai gives us the chance to incorporate the beauty of nature into our daily life. Those who grow and take care of bonsai trees have a strong connection to nature. They learn more about the complex interactions between trees, the changing of the seasons, and the environment. Spending time with their trees, seeing them grow, and taking in the natural cycles brings comfort and serenity to bonsai enthusiasts.

A living art form that encourages tremendous creativity and self-expression is bonsai. Each bonsai tree is a special creation that the artist has sculpted and fashioned according to their vision and aesthetic preferences. In order to construct the compositions they like, bonsai enthusiasts are allowed to select from a wide range of tree species, pot designs, and design ideas. This artistic side of bonsai gives people a platform for self-expression and enables them to display their creative abilities and unique points of view.

Bonsai cultivation involves commitment, expertise, and knowledge. Practitioners of bonsai feel a sense of pride in their accomplishments as the trees grow and mature. It is deeply satisfying to see how a small, ordinary tree is transformed into a graceful and artistic work of art. Because they know they have fostered and assisted these miniature trees on their journey, bonsai enthusiasts take great pride in their skill to shape and take care of them.

Bonsai cultivation teaches essential values like perseverance and patience. The practice of bonsai teaches its practitioners to appreciate their trees' gradual growth. It serves as a constant prompt that development and mastery take time. Bonsai lovers acquire the patience to wait for results and the appreciation for the subtle changes that happen over the course of months and years. Beyond the bonsai tree itself, this patience-building technique can have a significant impact on other aspects of life.

Growing bonsai may be a very therapeutic experience. A break from the demands and anxieties of daily life is provided by working with bonsai trees. The concentrated attention needed to shape, prune, and maintain bonsai enables people to achieve a state of flow in which their minds are totally focused on the present. This contemplative component of bonsai offers a priceless opportunity for unwinding, relieving tension, and refreshing the mind. When caring for their trees, many bonsai enthusiasts experience comfort and a sense of peace.

Growing bonsai is a lifelong learning process that enhances one's horticultural knowledge. Bonsai enthusiasts learn about tree species, soil composition, pruning methods, and the particular requirements of various tree species. They hone their observational, analytical, and bonsai styling skills. These horticultural skills and knowledge go beyond bonsai trees and can be used in other gardening endeavors, enhancing the whole gardening experience.

The bonsai community is a thriving and encouraging group of enthusiasts who share a similar passion. Being a part of this group offers chances to interact with like-minded people, share expertise, and take part in workshops, exhibitions, and bonsai clubs. A sense of community and lifelong friendships are fostered by a common passion of bonsai. Bonsai enthusiasts gather together to celebrate their accomplishments, share knowledge, and motivate future bonsai practitioners.

Growing bonsai fosters environmental responsibility and enhances one's awareness for the environment. The interconnectedness of nature and humans is better understood by bonsai enthusiasts. They learn about the delicate equilibrium needed to support and nourish plant life. People that pursue bonsai horticulture frequently become more conscious of the environment and start using composting, water-saving techniques, and organic pest control. Bonsai enthusiasts may promote the preservation and protection of our natural environment by growing bonsai.

In conclusion, cultivating bonsai is a journey that gives many advantages and profoundly enhances our lives. The art of bonsai offers a singular path for developing one's self and expressing oneself, from promoting patience and awareness to nurturing creativity and a connection to nature. Combined with the sense of accomplishment and camaraderie, bonsai's therapeutic qualities make for an enjoyable and rewarding experience. Bonsai enthusiasts embark on a lifetime of exploration, beauty, and a heightened appreciation for the wonders of nature as they immerse themselves in the skill of nurturing these miniature trees.

CHAPTER I
Getting Started with Bonsai

Understanding the concept of bonsai

Growing miniature trees is the ancient art of bonsai, which combines horticulture with creative ideas and a deep understanding of nature. Growing miniature trees in pots is just one aspect of bonsai; it also represents a deep appreciation for the harmony and beauty found in nature. The idea of bonsai will be examined in depth in this section, along with its philosophical foundations, design ideas, and the profound connection it generates between people and nature.

In its purest form, bonsai is an art form that seeks to condense the essence of nature into a miniature representation through the use of living plants. The beauty and grace of full-sized trees in nature are embodied by bonsai trees, which are trained and skillfully shaped by artists, as opposed to traditional forms of art, which use static materials. Through a variety of procedures, including pruning, wiring, and shaping, bonsai trees are sculpted and styled to produce symmetrical and aesthetically pleasing compositions.

Harmony and balance are fundamental to the bonsai way of thinking. Balance between the tree's natural development patterns and the desired artistic vision is what bonsai artists seek to achieve. This way of thinking is influenced by Zen Buddhism and Japanese aesthetics, emphasizing the value of simplicity, asymmetry, and appreciation of nature's imperfections. The balance found in the natural world is reflected in the tranquility and serenity that bonsai trees are meant to create.

In the making and growing of bonsai, nature is essential. Artists who create bonsai meticulously study the natural development patterns of trees in an effort to imitate the grace and elegance of its larger counterparts. In order to keep bonsai trees healthy and vibrant, it is essential to understand how plants react to light, water, and other environmental factors. The varying seasons serve as a source of inspiration for bonsai enthusiasts as well. They use methods like defoliation and the choice of suitable containers to imitate how time and weather affect trees.

The design of visually appealing and artistically pleasing compositions is guided by bonsai design principles. These fundamental principles include the following:

The miniature form of bonsai is one of its distinguishing features. A harmonic composition must be created by maintaining a sense of proportion. Each component, including the tree, pot, and surrounding scenery, should have a harmonious relationship with one another. Despite its smaller size, the bonsai tree seems natural and balanced due to its proportional relationships.

Although asymmetry is frequently embraced in bonsai, maintaining a feeling of balance is important in bonsai design. A pleasant and harmonious composition will result by evenly distributing the tree's weight and visual components. Careful positioning of branches, foliage, and empty space can create a sense of balance. When applied, symmetry should be delicate and natural, increasing the bonsai's overall aesthetic appeal.

The movement and flow of bonsai trees should be reminiscent of their larger-scale natural counterparts. The sense of dynamic motion inside the constrained space of the bonsai pot is created by the curve of the trunk, the positioning of branches, and the flow of leaves. With the help of these components, a miniature version of a mature tree is given a sense of life and energy.

Negative space is a critical component of composition in bonsai design. The empty or open spaces of a composition are referred to as "ma" in Japanese aesthetics. Negative space gives the bonsai balance, contrast, and a sense of serenity, which is just as crucial as the actual bonsai pieces themselves. It improves the overall visual experience by allowing the viewer's eyes to rest and take in the beauty and nuances of the tree.

The harmony seen in nature is what bonsai design concepts are meant to imitate. The art of bonsai cultivation involves the careful consideration of scale, proportion, balance, movement, and negative space to produce miniature landscapes that capture the beauty and serenity of the natural world. The spirit of bonsai trees, which are miniature versions of their larger counterparts found in woods and mountains, should be one of calmness and serenity.

The vast array of shapes and forms that make up bonsai each represent a unique aspect of nature and artistic expression. Several popular bonsai designs include:

The bonsai tree grows with a straight trunk that gradually taper toward the apex in the formal upright style. This aesthetic captures the grace, majesty, and tenacity of a mature tree standing tall in the wild. It is one of the most traditional and well-liked bonsai types due to the controlled vertical growth, which symbolizes harmony and balance.

An easier-going, more natural form is introduced by the informal upright style. The tree's trunk has a little curvature that gives the impression of movement and vitality. This aesthetic captures the dynamic quality of a tree swaying in a light breeze by imitating the organic development patterns seen in nature. The informal upright style gives a more relaxed and approachable look that promotes serenity and a sense of connection with nature.

Slanting bonsai trees have distinctively slanted trunks that give the impression that they are growing on a mountaintop or enduring high winds. This aesthetic captures the vitality and toughness of trees coping with environmental difficulties. The composition is given a dynamic aspect by the tree's slanted trunk, which provides visual appeal and a sense of motion. Slanted bonsai trees represent the capacity to overcome challenges by evoking up a spirit of determination and flexibility.

The trunk of cascade bonsai trees flows downward, frequently extending below the level of the pot. This design symbolizes trees that grow on steep cliffs or close to water, where they adapt to the difficult environment by favoring downward growth. The cascading trunk, which symbolizes the flow of water or the spectacular settings where these trees thrive, gives the cascade style a feeling of grace and elegance.

The windswept aesthetic highlights the tenacity and persistence of trees by capturing the effects of heavy winds on them. The foliage and branches are purposefully made to look swept to one side, as if by strong breezes. The struggle and resilience of trees fighting against the forces of nature are depicted in this manner. Windswept bonsai trees radiate a feeling of fortitude, character, and the capacity to flourish under difficult circumstances.

The process of growing bonsai calls for perseverance, commitment, and a never-ending quest for mastery. Years, if not decades, are needed for bonsai trees to grow and mature. The correct conditions must be provided, and bonsai enthusiasts must diligently shape their trees over time. The art of bonsai teaches its practitioners the virtues of perseverance, observation, and the benefits of sustained commitment.

With origins in ancient China and Japan, bonsai has a deep cultural and historical significance. Each bonsai tree holds a feeling of ancestry and history, and the art of bonsai has been handed down through the generations. By participating in bonsai cultivation, devotees connect with the wisdom and knowledge of those who have come before them and become a part of a long-standing tradition.

A distinctive platform for creativity and self-expression is offered by bonsai. Each bonsai tree is an expression of the creator's creative sensibilities and vision. Bonsai enthusiasts are allowed to select tree species, container designs, and design components that speak to them personally. Practitioners of bonsai are able to express their feelings, experiences, and unique perspectives on nature and beauty by means of the shaping and styling of bonsai trees.

In conclusion, bonsai is a philosophy that extends beyond the practice of cultivating miniature trees. It symbolizes a deep respect for nature, a way of thinking about harmony and balance, and a unique way of expressing one's own vision. Bonsai is a journey that calls for endurance, skill, and a strong bond with nature. People can begin a lifelong pursuit of beauty, artistry, and the enduring force of nature by comprehending the concept of bonsai.

Choosing the right tree species for beginners

A intriguing and fulfilling activity that enables people to connect with nature and express their creativity is bonsai, the art of cultivating miniature trees. The proper tree species must be chosen when a beginner begins their bonsai journey. Each kind of tree has particular characteristics, needs for growth, and difficulties. The variables to take into account while selecting the best tree species for novices will be covered in this section, with a focus on the species' adaptability, growth patterns, and suitability for bonsai culture.

It's crucial for beginners to choose tree species that are tolerant and adaptable to a range of environmental circumstances. Some species are more tolerant and adaptable than others, and some thrive in particular temperatures. Consider cultivating species that are renowned for their toughness, ease of maintenance, and adaptability for bonsai gardening, such as the Chinese Elm (Ulmus parvifolia), Ficus (Ficus spp.), or Juniper (Juniperus spp.). Because they are tolerant of a variety of environments and have a forgiving nature, these species have a higher chance of success for beginners.

The growing characteristics of the species should be taken into account while selecting a bonsai tree for novices. Others have slower growth rates, making them easier for beginners to care. Some species have rapid growth, need frequent pruning and maintenance. Due to their modest growth rates, trees like the Japanese Maple (Acer palmatum) and Boxwood (Buxus spp.) enable beginners to progressively hone their pruning and styling abilities. Beginners can choose trees that match their skill level and dedication by being aware of the growth tendencies of various types.

Growing trees in small form is only one aspect of bonsai; the art form also attempts to capture the beauty and character of mature trees. Due of their traits, certain tree species naturally lend themselves to bonsai aesthetics. Bonsai enthusiasts frequently select species with small leaves, fascinating bark patterns, or distinctive branching structures, such as the Trident Maple (Acer buergerianum) or the Pine (Pinus spp.). These plants have characteristics that naturally enhance their aesthetic appeal and make it simpler to create desirable bonsai forms and patterns.

For the bonsai to remain healthy and vibrant over time, consideration of the temperature and surroundings is essential. Others are more versatile, whereas certain species do better in certain conditions. An important way to learn about a tree species' tolerance for heat, humidity, and sunlight is to look into its natural habitat. Beginners can provide the ideal growing conditions, minimize stress on the tree, and increase its chances of survival and success by choosing species that are compatible with the local climate.

Personal preferences and an emotional connection should not be ignored when choosing the best tree species for beginners, even though practical factors are quite important. Selecting a species that speaks to the particular bonsai cultivator will increase their overall satisfaction and dedication to the art. Bonsai cultivation is an intensely personal and aesthetic activity. Cultivating a personal relationship with the chosen species creates a deeper respect and dedication to its care and development, regardless of whether it is a species admired for its symbolism or a species associated with fond childhood memories.

For beginners starting their bonsai journey, choose the proper tree species is an essential first step. Beginners can make well-informed judgments that put them in a good position for success by taking into account aspects including adaptability, growth habits, aesthetic fit for bonsai, environmental adaptation, and personal connection. It's critical to keep in mind that bonsai cultivation is a learning process and that setbacks and difficulties are inevitable along the way. Beginners may nurture their bonsai trees, develop their talents, and uncover the artistry and beauty that bonsai has to offer by choosing species that are suitable to them and investing time and effort in their care.

Beginners will come across a wide variety of tree species as they go deeper into the world of bonsai, each with its own charms and difficulties. Take advantage of the opportunity to learn and develop alongside your chosen tree as you watch how it responds to various methods and maintenance routines. The bonsai tree will become a lifelong companion for you and lead you on a path of artistic expression, connection with nature, and personal development if you have patience, persistence, and a genuine respect for the beauty of nature.

Essential tools and equipment for bonsai cultivation

The cultivation of bonsai is a delicate and complex procedure that needs specific tools and equipment. With the help of these tools, bonsai enthusiasts may precisely and carefully shape, design, and care for their miniature trees. Each piece of equipment, from simple hand tools to more advanced equipment, has a specific use in the bonsai art. The primary tools and equipment needed for bonsai growth will be covered in this section, along with their uses, variations, and the significance of choosing high-quality tools.

Hand tools are among the many tools that are available, and they are essential for shaping, pruning, and caring for the fragile bonsai trees. The following are the fundamental hand tools that any bonsai enthusiast needs to have on hand. These tools, which range from pruning shears to wire cutters, enable bonsai artists to carefully sculpt and refine their miniature works of art.

The foundation of a bonsai artist's toolset is a pair of pruning shears, sometimes referred to as bonsai scissors or secateurs. These portable tools are used to prune roots, branches, and foliage. Pruning shears come in a variety of sizes and designs and have diverse cutting capabilities. Straight-edged shears offer clean, accurate cuts that let the bonsai artist shape it precisely. On the other hand, curved-edged shears are ideal for reaching complicated branches and hard-to-reach areas.

A specialized instrument called a concave branch cutter is used to cut branches and stubs from bonsai trees while reducing visible scars. Its distinctive concave cutting edge produces a circular wound that heals more easily and blends in perfectly with the natural contours of the tree. A concave branch cutter can be used by bonsai artists to generate a finely tuned taper and branch structure, boosting the tree's overall aesthetic appeal.

In bonsai cultivation, knob cutters—which resemble concave branch cutters in appearance—serve a special function. They are experts in removing knobs or other protrusions from bonsai tree branches or trunks. Knob cutters give bonsai artists the ability to accurately shape the tree and remove undesired bumps and imperfections with their precision cutting action. The clean angles and feminine curves of the bonsai's structure are largely due to the use of this tool.

Wire cutters are essential equipment for bonsai training and styling. Copper or aluminum wire is frequently used to shape and direct branches into desirable locations while designing a bonsai tree. When it's time to cut the wire without causing any harm, wire cutters come to the rescue. These cutters are equipped with short, strong blades that can securely cut through wire of various gauges without endangering the tree.

The procedure of repotting requires the use of root pruning shears, commonly referred to as root cutters or root scissors. To keep bonsai trees healthy and from getting too crowded as they expand, their roots require regular pruning. When using root pruning shears, the bonsai artist can carefully trim the roots and keep a strong root system since the shears' strong, sharp blades make clean cuts. This encourages ideal nutrient absorption and ensures the tree's overall health.

Even the smallest details count in the world of bonsai cultivation. Tweezers are essential instruments for accomplishing precise operations because of their slender and sensitive shape. They help with weeding, clearing away trash, and precisely placing little cables or branches. Better maneuverability is provided by tweezers with angled or curved tips, which make them perfect for delicate work in the small bonsai pot.

Basic bonsai cultivation techniques such as shaping and styling enable artists to turn ordinary trees into living pieces of art. Here are a few of the key tools used in bonsai tree shape and styling.

A bonsai artist's arsenal must include bonsai wire. Branches may be shaped and placed precisely, giving them the required shape and form. Wires made of aluminum and copper are frequently used in bonsai, and they come in various gauges to accommodate varied branch thicknesses. Intricate branch structures can be made by artists by carefully wrapping the wire around branches and gently bending them. When it's time to cut the wire, wire cutters come in handy to make sure the branches are firmly in place.

During the style process, bonsai pliers, sometimes referred to as bonsai branch benders or jin pliers, are crucial instruments for exerting pressure and bending branches. Strong jaws and rounded edges of these pliers minimize damage to the sensitive bark or cambium layer. Artists may arrange branches precisely, create the appropriate shape and structure for the bonsai tree, and apply fine control and leverage with the help of bonsai pliers.

For making deadwood characteristics on bonsai trees, specialist tools called jin pliers and jin knives are employed. Jin alludes to the organic deadwood regions that give a tree character and age. Jin pliers have pointed points made for removing bark, which results in the creation of realistic deadwood areas. They give artists the opportunity to manipulate the deadwood and give it a natural look. While carving detailed details and textures into the deadwood with Jin knives, which have narrow, curved blades, can improve the tree's overall aesthetic appeal.

Regular maintenance and care are necessary for bonsai trees, including keeping the leaves, branches, and trunk clean and in good condition. With their tiny, pointed teeth, bonsai rakes are delicate tools used to rake and loosen the soil surface. They assist in clearing away weeds, trash, and moss without upsetting the bonsai tree's fragile roots. To clean the leaves, branches, and trunk, bonsai brushes, often composed of soft bristles or horsehair, are employed. They contribute to maintaining the tree's overall health and attractiveness by removing dirt, dust, and dead foliage.

It takes meticulous planning and close attention to detail while potting and displaying bonsai trees. The fundamental equipment for potting and displaying bonsai trees are listed below. They help with the overall aesthetics and maintenance of these little works of art.

A variety of shapes, sizes, and materials are available for bonsai pots, which are essential for the growth and display of bonsai trees. These containers offer a setting that promotes root development, makes drainage easier, and upholds aesthetic balance. Because of their resilience, insulating capabilities, and moisture retention capabilities, ceramic pots are frequently used. They provide solidity and a genuine appearance that enhance the bonsai craftsmanship. As a cheap substitute, plastic pots offer a lightweight, portable solution and are frequently used for pre-bonsai or young trees.

For bonsai trees to develop healthily, a particular mixture known as "bonsai soil" is required. It is carefully constructed to offer the best circumstances possible for root growth, including appropriate drainage, aeration, and water retention. Typically, bonsai soil is made up of an even mixture of inorganic and organic materials, such as perlite or pumice, and organic materials like compost, peat moss, or bark. Due to this composition, waterlogging is avoided while roots may access nutrients and oxygen in the soil. The bonsai tree's general vigor and lifespan are supported by the well-balanced growing medium.

A root hook comes in help during the repotting process for delicately loosening and combing out the roots of a bonsai tree. Without causing damage, it helps to separate the roots and remove the old soil. The root hook's curved, pointed points enable exact penetration into the root ball and provide gentle manipulation without causing damage to the fragile root system. This device is essential for preserving the roots' good health and encouraging successful repotting.

Watering bonsai trees is best done with a watering can that has a fine, narrow spout. It makes it possible to water precisely and strategically, ensuring that water reaches the root zone without disturbing the nearby soil or vegetation. Use a watering can with a rose attachment or a fine mesh to provide even water distribution and prevent soil erosion. This makes sure that water is released under control, keeping the proper level of moisture for the bonsai tree's health.

When styling, trimming, or displaying a bonsai tree, a turntable, often referred to as a bonsai stand or a lazy Susan, provides a revolving platform that makes it easier to reach all sides of the tree. It reduces the chance of damage and offers convenience for the artist by doing away with the necessity to reposition the tree all the time. The turntable makes it possible to see the bonsai tree completely from a variety of angles, promoting accurate craftsmanship and guaranteeing that all areas of the tree are given equal attention.

The artistic splendor of bonsai trees is shown on a raised platform known as a bonsai display table. It improves the display overall, provides appropriate viewing angles, and adds visual appeal. Display tables can be made to order and available in a variety of materials, including metal, stone, or wood. These tables offer an eye-catching backdrop that draws attention to the bonsai's exquisite elegance and elicits appreciation.

Purchasing high-quality bonsai tools is essential for getting accurate, clear results and extending the life of the tools themselves. When trimming or styling a tree, cheap or inferior equipment may not have sharp edges, harming the tree. They could also be fragile and need to be replaced frequently.

It's crucial to choose tools made of high-quality materials, like carbon steel or stainless steel, while making your selection. These materials are long-lasting, rust-resistant, and keep their sharpness over time. Additionally, ergonomic handles make long bonsai sessions more comfortable and convenient.

To increase the lifespan of tools, regular maintenance is necessary. After each usage, tools should be cleaned and dried to avoid rusting. When necessary, tools should be sharpened to guarantee accurate and effective cutting. The tools are further shielded from harm by proper storage in a sterile and dry environment.

In conclusion, choosing the right tools and equipment is crucial for bonsai growing success. For simple maintenance and care, hand tools like pruning shears, concave branch cutters, and root pruning shears are essential. Using bonsai wire, pliers, and jin knives, among other shaping and styling tools, artists can produce one-of-a-kind, beautiful patterns. The appropriate growth and display of bonsai trees are facilitated by potting and display materials like bonsai pots, soil, and watering cans. Precision, longevity, and a satisfying bonsai experience are ensured by picking high-quality equipment and attending to their care. With the proper equipment, bonsai enthusiasts can set out on an adventure of imagination, perseverance, and the development of miniature trees.

Setting up the perfect bonsai environment

For bonsai trees to flourish and maintain their overall aesthetic appeal, a perfect environment must be created. Due to its delicate nature and tiny stature, bonsai requires particular conditions in order to survive. We will look at the key components needed to create the ideal bonsai environment in this section. The significance of light, temperature, humidity, air circulation, and appropriate watering methods will be covered. The best environment for supporting the wellbeing of their trees can be created by bonsai enthusiasts by comprehending and putting these factors into practice.

One of the most important elements in the growth and development of bonsai is light. In order to perform photosynthesis, which is the mechanism by which bonsai trees transform light energy into chemical energy, they need a suitable balance of light. A sufficient amount of light exposure guarantees strong growth, beautiful colors, and healthy leaves. Here are some important things to think about:

The majority of bonsai plants grow in direct, strong light. Put your bonsai in a spot with at least six hours of direct sunlight every day. But take care because the midday sun can burn the vegetation. To shield your bonsai from extreme heat, move it or employ shading strategies.

Supplemental illumination is frequently required for indoor bonsai development, particularly in the winter when natural light is limited. The necessary light intensity and spectrum for ideal photosynthesis can be provided by LED grow lights or fluorescent lights with a spectrum suitable for plant growth. Place the lights close to the bonsai while keeping a safe distance to avoid burning it.

In order for bonsai trees to thrive and stay healthy, temperature is essential. The majority of bonsai trees prefer moderate temperatures, although different species have different requirements. Think about the following suggestions:

Seasonal temperature changes are advantageous for bonsai trees, especially those of the deciduous species. To recover and get ready for spring's fresh development, they need a dormant season throughout the winter, one with lower temperatures. Find out what temperature your particular tree species prefers, and then create the appropriate environment.

Bonsai trees can be harmed by extreme temperatures, whether they are hot or cold. Insulate your bonsai throughout the winter to prevent frost damage, or relocate it to a protected area. Direct heat sources, such as heaters or radiators, should be avoided because they can stress and dehydrate bonsai.

Think about the local climate where your bonsai is growing. Localized regions with marginally varied temperature and moisture conditions are referred to as microclimates. Observe how the temperature in your preferred area is impacted by things like buildings, fences, and neighboring bodies of water. To create the ideal environment, change the position of your bonsai accordingly.

For bonsai plants to stay healthy and vibrant, the right humidity levels must be maintained. varying climates around the world have varying humidity needs for bonsai trees. Here's how to achieve the perfect balance of humidity:

Your bonsai will have more humidity surrounding it if you set it on a humidity tray with water and rocks. The bonsai benefits from the microclimate of greater humidity that is created as the water evaporates. To prevent root rot, take care not to place the pot in the water directly.

Regularly misting the leaves of your bonsai can assist raise humidity levels, especially during dry periods or in low-humidity indoor conditions. To gently moisten the leaves while making sure not to flood the soil, use a fine mist sprayer.

Putting bonsai in a group might produce a microclimate with more humidity. Together, the trees transpire and release moisture into the atmosphere, which is advantageous to all of them. For species that flourish in increased humidity, such as tropical or subtropical kinds, this method is very beneficial.

For bonsai trees, proper air circulation is crucial as it helps avoid mold growth, stagnant air, and illness. The interchange of gases, a lower incidence of fungus infections, and healthy growth are all facilitated by enough ventilation. Think about the following techniques:

Air flow is often better in outdoor settings than it is indoors. If at all feasible, set your bonsai outside in good weather, making sure it is shielded from strong winds or extreme heat.

Make sure there is adequate airflow while growing bonsai indoors. To promote airflow and avoid the accumulation of stagnant air, open windows or turn on fans. Placement of bonsai should be avoided in confined areas with inadequate air circulation as this might result in moisture-related problems and fungus illnesses.

For bonsai to live and thrive, the right amount of watering is essential. Both overwatering and underwatering can be harmful to the health of the tree. Several important irrigation factors are listed below:

Numerous variables, such as tree species, pot size, soil type, and weather circumstances, affect how frequently plants need to be watered. It's critical to comprehend your bonsai tree's unique water requirements and modify your watering schedule accordingly. Regularly check the soil's moisture content by poking your finger or a moisture meter into it. Do not water before the soil surface begins to dry out.

Make sure the soil is well saturated before watering. Fill the pot with water until the extra runs out of the drainage holes at the bottom. Avoid soaking the surface exclusively, since this might result in uneven moisture distribution and shallow root growth. To avoid soil erosion or harm to fragile foliage, use a gentle watering can or nozzle attachment.

It is essential for bonsai cultivation to have well-draining soil. In addition to preventing soggy circumstances that might cause root rot, it enables optimal root aeration. Utilize a balanced bonsai soil mixture that offers sufficient drainage and holds on to enough moisture for the roots.

In conclusion, understanding and balancing a variety of parameters, such as light, temperature, humidity, air movement, and watering methods, is necessary to create the ideal bonsai environment. Bonsai enthusiasts can support the health, growth, and aesthetic appeal of their small trees by creating the ideal environment. Keep in mind to take into account the particular needs of your bonsai tree species and adapt the environmental conditions as necessary. Your bonsai will flourish and deliver pleasure and happiness for years to come with the right care and attention to the environment.

CHAPTER
II
The Art of Bonsai

Principles of bonsai design and aesthetics

In addition to being a horticultural practice, bonsai is also an expression of creativity and aesthetics due to its detailed and artistic display of miniature trees. Bonsai lovers can create aesthetically pleasing compositions by following the rules of bonsai design and aesthetics. Within the scope of this section, we will investigate the fundamental principles that govern the design of bonsai. We'll talk about ideas like balance, movement, harmony, simplicity, and symbolism. Bonsai enthusiasts can build engaging and emotive bonsai exhibits that capture the essence of natural beauty by comprehending and putting these ideas into practice.

In bonsai design, proportion, which refers to the relationship between the many components of the tree, pot, and overall composition, is a crucial principle. Harmony and balance are what we want to achieve. Think about the following proportional elements:

The bonsai tree's size must to be proportional to the pot's size. The height of the tree should ideally be six times the height of the pot, as a general guideline. With this ratio, the container and the tree are balanced visually.

The bonsai tree's branches ought to be in proportion to the trunk. Typically, thicker branches are located near the trunk's base, and finer branches are found near the apex. A sense of visual equilibrium and naturalness is produced by the progressive tapering.

Negative space, commonly referred to as void or empty space, is a crucial component of bonsai design. It alludes to the open spaces that encircle the tree and container. Making effective use of negative space contributes to the composition's overall harmony, balance, and sense of openness.

In a bonsai composition, the balance principle focuses on achieving visual equilibrium. To convey a sense of stability and harmony, it entails equally dispersing visual weight. In bonsai design, there are two primary types of balance:

When the elements on one side of the composition mirror those on the other, it is said to be in formal balance, also referred to as symmetrical balance. As a result, formality and stability are created. It is frequently employed in more formal and traditional bonsai forms.

A attractive composition can be created without exact symmetry by carefully arranging parts to produce informal equilibrium, commonly referred to as asymmetrical balance. It produces a more dynamic and organic look with a sense of flow and movement.

A bonsai composition should have harmony in order to create coherence and unity. In order to create a unified and aesthetically pleasing presentation, it entails taking into account the overall aesthetics, colors, textures, and shapes. Following are some crucial elements for attaining harmony:

When choosing and positioning your bonsai tree, take into account the colors of the foliage, flowers, bark, and pot. Aim for a color scheme that is harmonic and complimentary so that the composition will be aesthetically appealing and cohesive.

A variety of textures, including smooth and rough bark, delicate foliage, and coarser branches, can be seen on bonsai trees. A balanced and visually appealing presentation is produced by harmonizing the textures in the design. Think on the interaction between uneven and smooth surfaces as well as the contrast between fine and coarse textures.

The tree's shape, its branches, and its foliage should all complement and blend with one another. Think about the tree's overall silhouette, the branching structures, and the harmony of positive and negative space. Shapes that are in harmony produce a sense of coherence and flow.

A bonsai composition can be given a sense of dynamic and energy by implementing the principle of movement. In order to create the impression of natural movement and flow, branches, foliage, and other materials must be carefully arranged. Think about the following elements of movement creation:

To give the bonsai tree a feeling of movement and vitality, the trunk should have natural curves, bends, or twists. Avoid trunks that are tight and straight since they can appear dead and static.

Put the branches in a position that conveys motion and direction. Create soft curves and angles that resemble the natural growth patterns of trees by using methods like wiring and pruning.

The foliage should flow naturally with the branches to give the impression of movement and direction. Avoid arranging greenery in a consistent and symmetrical way because it may look stiff and manufactured.

The concept of simplicity places an emphasis on grace, minimalism, and the removal of extraneous components. In order to produce a clear and uncluttered composition, elements must be placed intentionally and thoughtfully. Think about the following simplicity-related elements:

To give the bonsai tree a sophisticated and elegant silhouette, prune its branches and foliage. Eliminate any extra branches or vegetation that takes away from the overall appearance.

Select bonsai containers with simple designs that don't overwhelm the tree. Don't use containers with elaborate decorations or patterns that distract from the bonsai's inherent beauty.

Make good use of negative space to convey a sense of simplicity and elegance. Allow the tree and pot to breathe and stand out by not packing the composition with too many elements.

Through the use of the symbolism principle, bonsai enthusiasts can express sentiment, meaning, and cultural relevance in their creations. Incorporating symbols with personal or cultural significance gives the bonsai display depth and a narrative. Think about the following symbolism elements:

Bonsai trees can serve as a symbol of cultural traditions and values. To add more depth and significance to your compositions, learn about the cultural meanings connected to particular tree species.

Bonsai can serve as a vehicle for the expression of one's feelings, memories, or experiences. Think about including items in your bonsai exhibit that have special meaning for you, including stones, figurines, or other symbolic items.

The beauty and symbolism of each season can be displayed through the design of bonsai displays, which can change as the seasons do. To improve the aesthetic impact and indicate the passage of time, think about including seasonal items like flowers, fruits, or autumn foliage.

In conclusion, the bonsai design and aesthetics principles offer a framework for producing aesthetically pleasing and unified compositions. The principles of proportion, balance, harmony, movement, simplicity, and symbolism can be used by bonsai enthusiasts to transform their creations from simple potted trees into living pieces of art. Keep in mind that these guidelines can be tailored and interpreted to suit unique preferences and creative expression rather than being absolute laws. Bonsai lovers can produce stunning bonsai displays that bring about inspiration and awe with practice and a profound respect for the innate beauty of trees.

Techniques for shaping and pruning bonsai trees

In bonsai cultivation, shaping and pruning are crucial methods that enable enthusiasts to sculpt and perfect the form of their trees. Aesthetically pleasant and visually striking compositions can be made by bonsai artists by carefully adjusting the branches, foliage, and overall structure. We will look at several shaping and pruning methods for bonsai plants in this section. Wiring, pruning, pinching, defoliation, and carving techniques will be covered. Bonsai enthusiasts can enhance their artistic vision and produce amazing bonsai exhibits by learning and using these techniques.

The branches and trunks of bonsai trees are guided and shaped using a method called wiring. To manage the direction and position of the branch or trunk's growth, a flexible wire is wrapped around it. The main features of wiring are as follows:

Based on the size and flexibility of the branch or trunk, choose the wire gauge and substance that are acceptable. Thinner wire is typically used for fragile branches and heavier wire for larger branches and trunks. Copper or aluminum wire is also frequently employed.

Make sure the anchor is secure but not too tight as you begin by securing the wire at the branch or trunk's base. Make sure the wire is uniformly spaced and in contact with the wood before gently wrapping it in a spiral pattern. Crossing wires should be avoided because they may be damaged or hinder growth.

When the tree is actively growing, which is often in spring or early summer, is the optimal time to wire branches. To avoid the wire slicing into the bark, keep an eye on the growth and adjust the wire as necessary. To prevent wire scarring, remove the wire after a few months.

In order to modify the tree's shape and structure, pruning is a crucial bonsai cultivation technique that entails carefully eliminating branches and foliage. Pruning aids in shaping the appropriate silhouette, ramification, and growth control. Take into account the following pruning methods:

Remove specific branches that interfere with the overall balance or take away from the desired form. Just above a leaf node or dormant bud, make a clean cut using bonsai pruning shears or concave cutters.

Take into account the branch's shape, width, and overall balance in the composition.

To promote lateral branching and produce a more compact and balanced profile, prune the leading or apical branch. By using this method, the tree's energy is distributed more evenly throughout it, and excessive vertical growth is prevented.

In order to encourage ramification and encourage the growth of lateral buds, pinching entails removing the terminal bud or bud pair. To help the tree grow a dense canopy and finer branching, pinch back new shoots to the desired length.

For deciduous bonsai trees, defoliation is a process used to improve ramification and perfect the tree's overall proportion. It entails the methodical removal of leaves in order to promote new growth and decrease leaf size. Take into account the following defoliation factors:

When the tree has fully leafed out in the late spring or early summer, defoliation is normally carried out. Defoliating weak or recently transplanted trees should be avoided since it may stress them.

Cutting the leaf stalk or petiole with care will allow you to remove the leaves while protecting the buds and emerging shoots. To prevent hurting the bud, keep a small part of the petiole attached to the stem.

After defoliation, the tree should be given the best conditions possible to recover and produce new leaves. Make sure the tree is properly watered, fertilized, and shielded from strong wind and sunlight. Within a few weeks, new, often smaller-sized leaves will appear, improving the proportion of the tree as a whole.

Bonsai enthusiasts can use carving to give the trunk and branches of their trees personality, texture, and aesthetic intrigue. To make hollows, jins (deadwood), and other artistic elements, the wood must be carefully removed or manipulated. Think about the following carving elements:

To remove or shape the wood, use the proper carving tools, such as chisels, gouges, and rotary tools. To provide clear and accurate results, make sure the tools are sharp and properly maintained.

Use carving techniques to give texture to the surface, hollow out portions of the trunk or branches, or make deadwood characteristics. Exercise caution to prevent causing harm to the tree's living tissues.

To prevent decay and pests, apply a sealant or preservative to the exposed wood. Additionally, to improve the appearance of deadwood features, think about applying lime sulfur or other wood-preserving substances.

In conclusion, bonsai enthusiasts can transform their trees into living works of art by using shaping and pruning procedures, which are important to the art. The form, structure, and texture of their trees can be changed by bonsai artists using techniques including wiring, pruning, pinching, defoliation, and carving, resulting in mesmerizing compositions that capture the beauty and essence of nature. When using these methods, it's crucial to do so with caution, understanding, and patience while constantly keeping in mind the tree's health and vitality. Bonsai enthusiasts can master the art of shaping and pruning, taking their bonsai creations to new levels of beauty and artistic expression, with practice and a keen eye for aesthetics.

Wiring and styling your bonsai

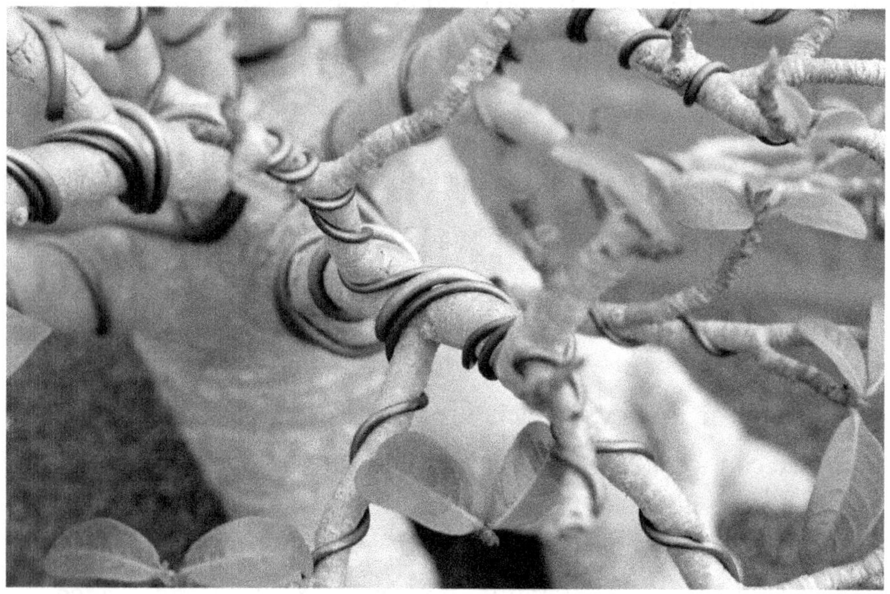

In order to shape and guide the growth of their trees and turn them into living works of art, bonsai enthusiasts use fundamental procedures called wiring and styling. While style entails the purposeful arrangement of branches, foliage, and other features to produce an aesthetically pleasing composition, wiring offers a way to manipulate the branches and trunks. In this section, we are going to delve into the wiring and styling techniques that are used in bonsai. Wiring's significance, how wires are applied, style considerations, and the role of artistic interpretation will all be covered. The ability to comprehend and master these methods will enable bonsai enthusiasts to produce distinctive and alluring bonsai designs that convey their aesthetic vision.

In bonsai cultivation, wiring is a crucial method that enables enthusiasts to form their trees' branches and trunks in accordance with their desired aesthetic goals. Wiring is necessary for the following reasons in particular:

The location and direction of branches may be precisely controlled by means of wiring, making it easier to create beautiful and well-balanced compositions. It enables the bonsai tree's general structure and form to be improved by the manipulation of angles, curves, and spacing.

Wiring allows bonsai artists to control the direction in which branches develop, giving the design movement and flow. This method aids in simulating the organic development patterns of trees, adding energy and authenticity.

Bonsai enthusiasts can foster the growth of secondary and tertiary branches, leading to finer ramification, by carefully wiring and arranging branches. As a result, the canopy becomes more detailed and refined, giving the bonsai design additional depth and visual intrigue.

It takes accuracy, perseverance, and knowledge of the tree's development tendencies to wire-frame bonsai trees. To apply wire successfully, follow these steps:

Depending on the size and flexibility of the branches or trunks, choose a wire gauge that is suitable. Thinner wire is typically used for fragile branches and heavier wire for larger branches and trunks. Copper or aluminum wire is also frequently employed. Take into account the appropriate level of flexibility and strength.

When adding wires to bonsai trees, timing is essential. Wire should ideally be used when the tree is actively growing, which is often in the spring or early summer. As a result, the wire may direct the growth and mold it into the appropriate shape before it solidifies.

Start by securing the wire to the branch or trunk's base. Make sure the anchor is stable but not too tight. Make sure the wire is evenly spaced and in contact with the wood as you carefully spiral-wrap it around the branch or trunk. Crossing wires should be avoided because they may be damaged or hinder growth.

Wires should be taken down when necessary to prevent slicing into the bark and leaving scars. Regularly check on the tree's development and get rid of the wire before it becomes embedded. This is normally carried out a few months after the wire was applied.

The deliberate placement of branches, foliage, and other components to produce an aesthetically pleasing and harmonious bonsai composition is known as styling. Keep the following things in mind when styling your bonsai:

The goal of bonsai styling should be to closely resemble tree growth in nature. Study how trees develop in their natural environments and take into account characteristics unique to each species. This knowledge will direct how the branches are arranged, how realistically the tapering is made, and how a balanced and organic design is created.

Consider how your styling choices will affect design principles like proportion, balance, harmony, and movement. Make sure the tree's overall form is aesthetically pleasant, with an evenly distributed canopy and balanced branch placement.

Effectively utilize negative space to add aesthetic appeal and draw attention to the tree's attributes. Areas of empty space or open space within the composition are referred to as negative space. Make sure there is enough area between the branches and the foliage so that each may breathe and stand out.

Personal artistic expression is also a part of bonsai styling. Don't be hesitant to add your own distinctive style and imagination to the composition while still sticking to design principles and natural aesthetics. Create a bonsai that matches your artistic vision by experimenting with various branch placements, angles, and overall forms.

In the cultivation of bonsai, styling and wiring are ongoing activities. To maintain and improve the bonsai tree's design, regular maintenance and improvement are required. Think about the following:

To keep the bonsai tree's shape, promote ramification, and perfect the design, prune it regularly. Eliminate any extraneous branches or foliage that takes away from the composition as a whole.

Additionally, regular pruning guarantees that the bonsai maintains its proportion as it develops.

Keep an eye on the wired branches and make any necessary changes. The wire can start to get too tight or start to rip into the bark as the branches get bigger and thicker. Before it causes harm, loosen or cut the wire, and then replace it as necessary.

Review your bonsai tree's styling on a regular basis. It may be necessary to make adjustments as the tree grows and changes in order to preserve its aesthetic balance and overall integrity. Style selections must change and develop with the tree.

In conclusion, bonsai enthusiasts can shape and direct the growth of their trees using wiring and styling, which is a transformative approach that enables them to realize their artistic ambitions. Bonsai artists can precisely regulate the positioning, direction, and shape of the branches and trunks by carefully applying wires. Bonsai trees can be styled to produce aesthetically pleasing and unified compositions by taking into account design principles, natural aesthetics, and individual artistic interpretation. The development and preservation of the bonsai design are ensured by regular maintenance and improvement. Bonsai enthusiasts may master the skills of wiring and styling, producing distinctive and alluring bonsai displays that showcase their enthusiasm and creativity, with persistence, practice, and a profound appreciation for the art.

Choosing the right pot and repotting techniques

Vital aspects of bonsai cultivation include selecting the proper pot and comprehending the repotting procedure. In addition to functioning as a practical container for the tree, the pot also adds beauty to the composition as a whole. Repotting, on the other hand, protects the bonsai's health and vitality by allowing for correct draining and providing the space required for root growth. The significance of selecting the appropriate pot, the factors to be taken into account while repotting, and advice on repotting procedures will all be covered in this section. Making informed judgments and ensuring the long-term success of their trees are made easier for bonsai enthusiasts by being aware of these factors.

A bonsai tree's pot selection involves more than just aesthetic considerations. Choosing the proper pot is essential for the following reasons:

The pot should be appropriate for the bonsai tree's size and aesthetic. While preserving a balanced and harmonic relationship with the tree's general structure, it should allow enough room for root growth. The roots may be restricted by a pot that is too small, while the delicate beauty of the tree may be overwhelmed by a pot that is too large.

Ceramic, plastic, or clay are the main materials used to make bonsai pots. Each material offers advantages and things to keep in mind. Plastic pots are lightweight and offer excellent insulation, whereas ceramic pots are preferred for their longevity and aesthetic appeal.

Clay pots can dry out more quickly yet they are porous and encourage airflow to the roots.

For bonsai trees to stay healthy, proper drainage is essential. To let excess water to drain and prevent waterlogged soil, which can cause root rot, the pot should contain drainage holes. Consider the pot's design as well and make sure it allows for adequate airflow around the roots.

The pot should enhance the tree's overall presentation and go well with the tree's design. Think about elements like shape, color, and texture to make sure the pot highlights the tree's inherent beauty and achieves the intended aesthetic.

Repotting is a crucial step in bonsai cultivation that supports healthy roots, prevents soil compaction, and ensures proper nutrient absorption. When deciding whether to repot a bonsai tree, keep the following things in mind:

Repotting usually takes place when the tree is dormant or just starting to grow. This typically occurs in the early spring, before the buds enlarge. Repotting at this time enables the tree to heal and develop new roots before to the start of the growing season.

Make sure the tree's roots are in good condition before repotting to determine whether it has to be done. Search for overpopulation indicators like circular or densely packed roots. Firm, white, and equally distributed throughout the root ball indicate healthy roots.

Pruning the roots during repotting is necessary to promote new development and keep a small root system. To cut off any roots that are too long or have damage, use sharp bonsai root pruning shears. In order to ensure that only a portion of the root mass is removed, prune the roots back in a balanced way.

For bonsai health, choosing the right soil substrate is essential. A balance of moisture retention and drainage should be present in bonsai soil. Use a bonsai-specific soil blend that drains well and encourages ventilation and nutrient uptake. A standard garden soil should not be used because it can retain too much moisture and suffocate the roots.

Knowing how to properly repot bonsai trees ensures a smooth transition and encourages strong root development. For appropriate repotting, adhere to these guidelines:

The new pot, bonsai soil mixture, wire (to hold the tree in the pot), and bonsai root pruning shears should all be gathered before repotting. To make sure the new pot is well hydrated, soak it in water.

Gently loosen the dirt and untangle any roots that may be encircling the root ball before carefully removing the bonsai tree from its present container. Take care not to harm the vulnerable root system.

To maintain a compact root system, inspect the roots and prune them back. Ensure a balance between the root mass and the foliage by removing any broken, diseased, or excessively long roots.

In the bottom of the new pot, add a layer of bonsai soil mixture, then place the tree in the center. More soil should be added around the roots, and it should be carefully worked into any gaps to ensure proper contact. Use bonsai wire to secure the tree in the pot and hold it upright and steadily.

Water the tree well after repotting to help the soil surrounding the roots settle. For a few weeks, place the bonsai in a shaded spot to reduce stress on the roots. During this time, keep a close eye on the tree's watering requirements.

In conclusion, two crucial parts of bonsai cultivation are selecting the appropriate pot and understanding the repotting procedure. The bonsai tree's aesthetic appeal is improved by the pot in addition to its practical use as a container. Repotting, on the other hand, protects the tree's health and vitality by allowing enough room for root development and encouraging correct drainage. When choosing a pot, bonsai enthusiasts can provide their trees with the best environment possible by taking into account elements like size, material, drainage, and aesthetics. In the same way, utilizing the right repotting methods—including timing, root assessment, pruning, and the use of the proper soil substrate—will encourage healthy root development and overall tree development. Bonsai enthusiasts can guarantee the long-term success and beauty of their bonsai trees by taking careful consideration and following appropriate procedures.

CHAPTER
III
The Science of Bonsai

Understanding the biology of trees in bonsai cultivation

An in-depth knowledge of tree biology is necessary for successful bonsai development. Bonsai enthusiasts can cultivate a holistic approach to their cultivation practices by learning about the complex inner workings of trees, assuring the health, vigor, and lifespan of their bonsai specimens. The fundamental elements of tree biology that are essential to bonsai cultivation will be discussed in this section. We will go through the structure of trees, photosynthesis and transpiration processes, the function of hormones in controlling growth, and the effects of changing seasons. Understanding these basic biological concepts will enable bonsai enthusiasts to make wise decisions, give their bonsai trees the care they need, and cultivate ideal growing circumstances.

It is crucial to comprehend the anatomical structure of trees in order to understand the biology of trees used in bonsai cultivation. Important tree anatomy features that apply to bonsai include as follows:

The trunk serves as the center of the tree's structure and support. The bonsai's thickness, taper, and bark texture all add to the tree's overall beauty. The age of the tree can also be ascertained by analyzing the growth rings in the trunk.

From the trunk, branches protrude and are crucial for nutrient transport and photosynthesis. The canopy and quantity of foliage on the bonsai are supported by them. Pruning and wiring methods are aided by knowledge of branch development, attachment angles, and apical dominance.

Photosynthesis, the process through which trees turn sunlight, carbon dioxide, and water into energy, depends critically on leaves. Different tree species have different leaves in terms of size, shape, color, and texture, which affects how the bonsai looks as a whole.

The tree's roots take up water and nutrients and hold the tree in the ground. Understanding root growth patterns, radial nebari development, and root pruning methods is essential for keeping healthy, properly proportioned plants in bonsai culture.

The cultivation of bonsai depends heavily on the fundamental biological processes of photosynthesis and transpiration in trees. Understanding these procedures enables bonsai enthusiasts to give their trees the best possible care and surroundings.

The process by which trees produce glucose (energy) and oxygen from sunlight, carbon dioxide, and water is known as photosynthesis. Chlorophyll, a substance found in leaves, absorbs sunlight and starts the chemical processes required for photosynthesis. To sustain wholesome growth and maintain energy reserves, bonsai plants need to be exposed to enough light.

Water vapor is expelled from tree leaves and stems by transpiration. On the surface of the leaf, it takes place through tiny openings known as stomata. Transpiration, which generates a suction force that sucks water up from the roots, is essential for water and nutrient intake. For bonsai trees to avoid dryness and maintain healthy transpiration rates, proper watering and humidity management are crucial.

In order to control the growth and development of trees, hormones are extremely important. Understanding how they work enables bonsai practitioners to monitor growth patterns, promote branching, and regulate tree size.

Auxins are hormones that cause apical dominance, a condition in which a tree's apical bud prevents the development of lateral buds. A bonsai enthusiast can deliberately pinch back or prune the apical bud to promote lateral branching and produce the ideal tree shapes by knowing the function of auxins.

Cytokinins affect bud formation and encourage cell division. Bonsai enthusiasts can control bud growth, encourage ramification, and create balanced tree structure by adjusting cytokinin levels through pruning, grafting, or hormone injections.

Gibberellins are hormones that control internode length and cell elongation. Bonsai enthusiasts can control tree proportions and encourage compact development in some species by being aware of their effects.

Seasonal variations have a big impact on the development and growth of trees in bonsai horticulture. Understanding these seasonal changes enables bonsai enthusiasts to modify their maintenance procedures.

The winter months are a time of dormancy for many tree species. By recognizing dormancy, bonsai enthusiasts can modify their watering, fertilizer, and trimming routines to create the ideal environment for the tree to rest and regenerate.

Trees experience a period of rapid growth in the spring. For this active growth stage, bonsai enthusiasts should concentrate on supplying enough light, fertilizers, and water.

Summer necessitates careful attention to watering since bonsai trees can quickly become dry due to higher temperatures and evaporation rates. It can also be required to shield the tree from direct sunlight and provide sufficient shade.

Numerous tree species display vibrant foliage color changes in the fall. By providing the right lighting and changing watering procedures, bonsai enthusiasts can improve the bonsai's appearance. The bonsai needs to be protected from cold temperatures, powerful winds, and heavy wetness throughout the winter months.

In conclusion, successful bonsai cultivation depends on a grasp of tree anatomy. It is possible for bonsai enthusiasts to provide their trees the proper care and cultivate ideal growing circumstances by being knowledgeable about the anatomy of trees, the processes of photosynthesis and transpiration, the function of hormones, and the effects of seasonal variations. By putting this knowledge to use, bonsai enthusiasts may choose wisely when it comes to wiring, watering, fertilizing, and overall tree care. The ability to appreciate and master the art of bonsai is ultimately enhanced by a thorough understanding of tree biology, which enables the construction of beautiful and harmonious miniature trees.

Soil composition and proper watering techniques

For bonsai trees to be successfully grown, proper watering methods and soil composition are essential. For the health and growth of the tree, the ideal soil composition offers the nutrients, water retention, and drainage required. Additionally, knowing how to water properly ensures that bonsai trees get the right amount of moisture without running the risk of being overwatered or underwatered. In this section, we'll look at the significance of soil composition in bonsai cultivation, go over the elements of the perfect soil mixture, examine the value of appropriate watering methods, and offer advice on how to water bonsai trees. The ability to produce ideal growing circumstances for their trees and maintain their long-term health and vitality will enable bonsai enthusiasts to use these elements.

The health and development of bonsai trees are greatly influenced by the soil in which they are grown. For the cultivation of bonsai, soil composition is crucial for the following main reasons:

The main source of nutrients for bonsai trees is the soil. It offers the necessary components for growth, leaf development, and overall tree health. The availability of nutrients in a form that the tree can easily absorb is ensured by the proper soil composition.

A careful balance between water retention and drainage is necessary for bonsai trees. The soil should be able to retain moisture without getting waterlogged. In order to promote healthy growth, proper drainage prevents root rot and allows oxygen to reach the roots.

In bonsai trees, root development is directly influenced by the soil's composition. A soil mixture that drains properly promotes root development and guards against root suffocation or compaction. It enables roots to penetrate the soil and develop a solid, robust root system.

Water retention and drainage should be balanced in the appropriate soil mixture for bonsai growing. The following are the main elements of a well adjusted bonsai soil mix:

Inorganic components like lava rock, pumice, and akadama are frequently utilized in bonsai soil mixtures. A particular kind of clay called akadama is good at retaining water while also allowing for efficient drainage. Lava rock and pumice encourage airflow and minimize compaction, ensuring that the roots receive enough oxygen.

Organic components help the soil retain nutrients and encourage microbial activity. Examples include composted bark, peat moss, and sphagnum moss. These components supply organic matter that enhances the structure of the soil and the availability of nutrients.

Particles of different sizes are usually included in bonsai soil mixtures. This combination of coarse and fine particles encourages ideal drainage and water retention. While coarse particles promote water circulation and assist avoid waterlogging, fine particles aid in the retention of moisture.

Another crucial factor is the soil mixture's pH level. Most bonsai trees enjoy a pH range between slightly acidic and neutral. The soil mixture's pH level should be checked and adjusted as necessary to ensure that the tree's ability to absorb nutrients is not compromised.

The health and vitality of bonsai trees must be maintained through the use of appropriate watering methods. Key factors for efficient watering include the following:

Numerous variables, such as tree species, pot size, weather circumstances, and soil composition, affect how frequently plants need to be watered. As a general rule, water bonsai trees when the soil surface begins to dry out but before it fully dries out. Use a moisture meter or stick your finger into the soil to check the moisture levels.

Make sure the root ball is completely saturated while watering. Fill the pot with water until the water runs out of the drainage holes at the bottom. This encourages appropriate hydration and ensures that water reaches the entire root system.

When watering bonsai trees, be careful not to use too much force since this could disturb the soil and harm the fragile root structure. To properly disperse water, use a soft watering can or a fine misting nozzle. Sunburn and fungal infections can be avoided by misting the soil surface rather than the leaves directly.

Water quality is crucial while caring for bonsai trees. Use water that is devoid of chlorine if possible. If the tap water you want to use to water your bonsai trees has high levels of chlorine, let it sit in an open container for a few hours to let the chlorine evaporate.

Adapt your watering techniques to the changing seasons. Due to increased evaporation during the hot summer months, bonsai trees may need to be watered more frequently. Contrarily, limit watering during cooler months or dormant seasons to avoid overwetting the soil.

In conclusion, adequate watering methods and soil composition are essential components of bonsai cultivation. The ideal balance of water retention and drainage is provided by the correct soil mixture, enabling the best root growth and nutrient availability. Bonsai enthusiasts can create a favorable growing environment for their trees by comprehending the elements of an optimal soil mixture and their functions. A bonsai tree will receive the necessary amount of moisture without being overwatered or underwatered if you have mastered suitable watering practices. The health and vitality of their bonsai plants can be preserved by bonsai enthusiasts by considering elements like watering frequency, amount, techniques, and water quality. For years to come, bonsai enthusiasts can enjoy the beauty and lifespan of their miniature trees by using the right soil composition and efficient watering techniques.

Fertilization and nutrient management

Successful bonsai cultivation depends on managing nutrients and fertilization. To promote their development, health, and overall vitality, bonsai trees need a consistent supply of nutrients. Bonsai enthusiasts may deliver the necessary materials in the proper amounts at the right times by understanding the basics of fertilization and nutrient management. In this section, we'll look at the value of fertilization in bonsai cultivation, go over the essential nutrients bonsai trees need, examine various fertilizer types, and offer advice on good fertilization practices and nutrient management. Bonsai enthusiasts can assure ideal nutrient levels, encourage strong growth, and improve the aesthetic appeal of their bonsai plants by mastering these areas.

For bonsai trees, fertilization is vital since it replaces nutrients that may become depleted over time. The following points highlight the significance of fertilization in bonsai cultivation:

Comparatively to their counterparts in the ground, bonsai trees growing in containers have less access to natural nutrient sources. Nutrient deficiencies, which can result in stunted growth, yellowing leaves, and decreased overall vigor, can be avoided with regular fertilization.

The right fertilization supplies the nutrients needed for strong growth, including the growth of strong roots, branches, and foliage. It encourages healthy tree structure, strong shoots, and a mass of dense foliage.

The aesthetic appeal of bonsai trees depends on fertilization. It supports fine twig development, increases the production of dense ramification, and helps retain bright leaf color.

A variety of nutrients are necessary for bonsai plants to grow and thrive at their best. Effective nutrition management requires an understanding of the key nutrients and their functions. The essential nutrients that bonsai trees need are:

As it encourages the creation of chlorophyll, the pigment responsible for photosynthesis, nitrogen is essential for the growth of foliage. It encourages strong growth and a healthy, lush green canopy of leaves.

For plants to expand their roots, flower, and yield fruit, phosphorus is necessary. It improves the general health of the plant, encourages root development, and stimulates the flow of energy throughout the tree.

Potassium helps plants be more resilient to environmental challenges and maintain overall health. It boosts water uptake, increases disease resistance, and aids in nutrient absorption.

In smaller amounts, bonsai plants also need secondary nutrients like calcium (Ca), magnesium (Mg), and sulfur (S). These nutrients aid in the development of cell structures, the activation of enzymes, and the production of chlorophyll, among other physiological functions.

It is necessary to have trace amounts of micronutrients like iron (Fe), manganese (Mn), zinc (Zn), copper (Cu), molybdenum (Mo), and boron (B). These nutrients are essential for the operation of enzymes, nutrient absorption, and overall plant metabolism.

For bonsai cultivation, a variety of fertilizers are available, each with unique qualities and benefits. The best fertilizer for bonsai hobbyists' plants can be chosen by understanding the different types of fertilizers:

Organic fertilizers come from organic materials like seaweed, compost, manure, and bone meal. As they decompose, they steadily release nutrients over time, supplying a steady flow of nutrients. Organic fertilizers stimulate microbial activity, strengthen soil structure, and support long-term soil health.

Chemically prepared inorganic (synthetic) fertilizers deliver nutrients in easily absorbable forms. They provide exact nutrition ratio management and are quickly absorbed by the tree. Granules, powders, and liquid concentrates are just a few of the several formulations of inorganic fertilizers that are available.

Fertilizers with controlled release are made to release nutrients gradually over a long period of time. They are offered in coated granule or pellet form, allowing for a gradual and reliable administration of nutrients. For bonsai enthusiasts, controlled-release fertilizers offer a practical alternative and reduce the frequency of treatment.

Bonsai trees are given the appropriate nutrients in the right amounts due to efficient fertilization methods and nutrient management. For effective fertilization, keep the following in mind:

During the growing season, when the bonsai trees are actively in need of nutrients for growth, fertilize them. Early spring to late summer usually fall within this time frame. Depending on the particular requirements of the tree species, adjust the fertilization plan.

The manufacturer's recommendations for fertilizer application rates should be followed. Avoid making direct touch with the trunk or foliage as you evenly distribute the fertilizer across the soil's surface. Nutrient imbalances or root burn can result from overfertilization.

Following fertilization, water bonsai trees right away to guarantee optimum nutrient absorption and reduce the risk of root burn. Watering facilitates the uniform distribution of nutrients throughout the soil and promotes root uptake.

To precisely determine the tree's fertilizer needs, periodically test the soil's pH and nutrient content. Soil testing enables bonsai enthusiasts to modify fertilizing procedures according to the unique requirements of the tree.

Nutrient ratios may need to be adjusted depending on the bonsai tree's growth stage and unique requirements. For instance, fertilizers with a high nitrogen content are advantageous during the growth stage, whereas those with a higher phosphorus content can be appropriate for flowering or root development.

The addition of organic matter to the soil, in the form of compost or other organic fertilizers, helps to preserve the fertility of the soil over the long term and increases the amount of nutrients that are available.

Finally, it should be noted that proper fertilization and nutrient management are essential to bonsai cultivation success. It is possible for bonsai enthusiasts to feed their trees with the best nourishment by understanding the significance of fertilization, the essential nutrients that bonsai plants need, and the various forms of fertilizers. Bonsai enthusiasts can encourage vigorous development, improve the aesthetic appeal of their trees, and maintain their long-term health and vitality by adhering to proper fertilization practices, putting timing, application rates, and nutrient modifications into consideration. Bonsai trees flourish and the artistry of bonsai cultivation is completely realized through efficient fertilization management.

Dealing with pests and diseases in bonsai trees

The health and vitality of bonsai trees are seriously threatened by pests and diseases. If left untreated, these unwanted guests may harm the tree's leaves, impair its structure, and possibly cause the tree to die. The health of bonsai trees must therefore be maintained by being aware of common diseases and pests that affect them, taking preventative measures, and using efficient treatment techniques. We will address typical pests and illnesses encountered, look into preventive measures, and offer advice on how to properly deal with infestations and diseases as we examine the significance of pest and disease control in bonsai culture. We can preserve the long-term health and resilience of bonsai trees by arming enthusiasts with information and tactics.

Management of pests and diseases is essential in bonsai cultivation for a number of reasons:

The entire health of bonsai trees can be compromised by pests and diseases, which can result in stunted growth, defoliation, and even death. Trees can survive and grow if proper pest and disease management techniques are used.

For its aesthetic value and beauty, bonsai trees are valued. The aesthetic qualities of the tree may be diminished as a result of infestation by pests and diseases, which may result in discoloration of the leaves, deformation of the leaves, or damage to the tree's overall structure. The aesthetic appeal of bonsai trees can be preserved through proactive management.

Pests and diseases have a tendency to spread quickly, harming nearby plants in addition to the affected tree. Bonsai enthusiasts can avoid the spread of diseases and infestations to other trees and reduce possible harm by quickly managing them.

Numerous pests and illnesses can affect bonsai trees. The following are some of the most typical problems in bonsai cultivation:

Aphids, scale insects, mealybugs, spider mites, and caterpillars are a few of the insect pests that can infest bonsai trees. They damage the leaves, branches, and trunk as they feed on the foliage, sap, or wood. In extreme circumstances, they may impair the health of the tree as a whole.

Bonsai trees are susceptible to fungal diseases such powdery mildew, root rot, and numerous leaf spot diseases. If left untreated, these diseases can cause leaf wilting, death, and leaf discoloration since they flourish in humid environments.

Additionally vulnerable to bacterial and viral diseases are bonsai trees. These infections may result in leaf spots, cankers, stunted growth, and a general deterioration in tree health. To effectively manage viral and bacterial infections, prevention and early detection are crucial.

In order to reduce pest and disease problems in bonsai plants, prevention is essential. The following are crucial precautions to take:

By routinely eliminating weeds, debris, and fallen leaves, you can keep the area around your bonsai neat and orderly. This lessens the number of areas where bugs could hide and gets rid of potential illness sources.

Quarantine new bonsai trees or plant material for a while to look for any signs of pests or illnesses before adding it to your collection. Check trees frequently for signs of illness or infestation.

Place bonsai trees in places that are suitable for them, with enough sunlight and airflow, and without being too crowded. In ideal circumstances, healthy trees are more resistant to pests and diseases.

In order to prevent fungal illnesses, proper watering techniques are essential. Avoid overwatering because it can encourage the growth of fungi. Instead of spraying the foliage, water the soil directly to lower the danger of leaf diseases.

To avoid waterlogging, which can cause root rot and other fungal illnesses, make sure the soil is properly draining. Use soil mixtures ideal for bonsai growing that drain properly.

By providing sufficient fertilization, you can maintain a good nutrient balance and support the health and resilience of your trees. Healthy trees are better able to tolerate pressure from pests and diseases.

Infestations of pests and diseases are still possible despite precautions. Here are some practical solutions for overcoming these difficulties:

Determine the specific pest or disease that is damaging your bonsai tree. This process is essential for choosing the best treatment strategy.

In other instances, manually eliminating pests—such as hand-picking caterpillars or removing scale insects—can offer relief right away.

Manage insect pests by using natural pest management techniques like insecticidal soaps, neem oil, or horticultural oils. These approaches for managing pests without harming beneficial insects are generally secure and efficient.

Chemical fungicides or insecticides may be used as necessary. To reduce potential damage to the tree, the environment, and helpful insects, use caution when applying these items and pay close attention to the directions.

Implement integrated pest management (IPM), which incorporates cultural behaviors, preventive measures, and selective treatment strategies. IPM places a strong emphasis on using eco-friendly tactics to efficiently manage diseases and pests.

When dealing with severe pests or illnesses, seek guidance from knowledgeable bonsai enthusiasts, horticulturists, or arborists. Depending on their level of experience, they can offer specific recommendations or guidance on appropriate treatment approaches.

In conclusion, managing pests and diseases is essential to bonsai cultivation. The health and vitality of their trees can be preserved by bonsai enthusiasts by appreciating the value of preventative measures, identifying frequent pests and illnesses, putting preventive measures into practice, and using efficient treatment techniques. The general resiliency of bonsai trees is influenced by regular observation, good hygiene habits, appropriate tree location, and wholesome feeding. When infestations or diseases do arise, timely detection and the use of suitable management strategies, such as integrated pest management and organic pest control, contribute to the protection of the trees and maintain their visual attractiveness. Bonsai enthusiasts may take advantage of the enduring beauty and health of their valued bonsai trees by being proactive and using efficient pest and disease management techniques.

CHAPTER
IV
Bonsai Care and Maintenance

Seasonal care guidelines for bonsai

For bonsai trees to flourish and keep up their beauty throughout the year, specific attention and care are needed. The development, health, and overall well-being of bonsai trees are impacted by seasonal changes, demanding particular care procedures for each season. In this section, we'll look into the spring, summer, fall, and winter bonsai care recommendations. Bonsai enthusiasts can maintain the vitality and durability of their cherished trees by being aware of the particular requirements of bonsai trees during each season and using the proper care techniques.

For bonsai trees, spring is a time of active growth and renewal. The beginning of the year is a crucial time for laying the groundwork for the rest of the year. During this time, it's crucial to execute the following care techniques:

First, as the tree enters its development period in the spring, repotting is advised. Repotting enables for root maintenance, soil renewal, and year-round promotion of healthy development. Additionally, spring is a good time to wire and prune structures. Pruning increases ramification, shapes the tree, and cuts off undesirable branches. Wiring enables branches to be bent and shaped to produce desired bonsai forms.

Additionally, fertilization is crucial in the spring to supply the nutrients required for healthy growth. To support foliage development and general vigor, use balanced fertilizers with a higher nitrogen content. Keep a close eye on the moisture levels in the soil and adjust watering as necessary. In order to keep the soil from drying out when the temperature rises, bonsai plants may need to be watered more frequently.

Last but not least, it's critical to frequently check trees for signs of pests and diseases. Apply preventive steps, such as clearing away fallen leaves, keeping good hygiene habits, and, if necessary, using organic pest control techniques.

Summertime brings warmer temperatures and more sunlight, which necessitates particular maintenance procedures to protect bonsai trees. Think about the following suggestions:

In order to avoid dehydration during the hot summer months, irrigation is of utmost importance. Water bonsai trees thoroughly and consistently, monitoring the moisture content of the soil frequently, and modifying the frequency of watering as necessary. To avoid sunburn and leaf scorch, bonsai plants must be given shade during the hottest portion of the day.

To maintain tree growth and general health, regular fertilization with a balanced fertilizer is required. Depending on the particular needs of the tree species, adjust the rate at which fertilizer is applied. During the summer, regular care and pruning are also crucial. By removing extra foliage, you can increase airflow and lessen water loss from transpiration. Keep a regular eye out for diseases and pests, and if you find any, take the necessary action.

For bonsai trees, autumn is a time of transition as they get ready for dormancy. During this time, it's vital to execute the following care techniques:

Autumn is the time to maintain your leaves. To keep things tidy and avoid moisture buildup, which can result in fungus illnesses, routinely remove fallen leaves. Early in the autumn season, use a balanced fertilizer to feed the tree with vital nutrients before it becomes dormant. This encourages root growth and gets the tree ready for the winter.

Light pruning should be done to keep the tree's shape and sick or dead branches should be removed. Heavy pruning should be avoided because it can encourage new growth that won't have enough time to harden off before winter. Bring bonsai trees indoors or give them enough insulation to protect them from frost. To avoid waterlogging and root rot, watering frequency should be varied based on temperature and rainfall.

For bonsai trees, winter is a time of dormancy, hence particular maintenance procedures are required to guarantee their life and wellbeing:

Place bonsai trees in a cold frame, greenhouse, or other protected area to protect them from freezing conditions. To shield the roots, use insulating materials like mulch or straw. During the winter, give bonsai trees only a little water to keep the soil just moist enough. Avoid overwatering because the tree needs less water now that its metabolism is less active.

Wintertime pruning should be kept to a minimum. To preserve the beauty and health of the tree, only remove dead or broken limbs. While some insects and pathogens may hibernate, keep an eye out for them on bonsai trees. Take the necessary precautions to ward off infections and infestations. Since the tree's metabolic processes slow down and there is less of a requirement for nutrients throughout the winter, fertilization should be reduced or stopped.

In conclusion, the effectiveness of bonsai cultivation depends on proper seasonal maintenance. The health, growth, and life of their trees can be ensured by bonsai enthusiasts by knowing and putting into practice the proper maintenance techniques for each season. Each season necessitates particular care, from springtime repotting and pruning to summertime insect control, fall dormancy preparation, and wintertime protection. Bonsai enthusiasts may create an environment that promotes the growth and flourishing of their treasured bonsai trees by adhering to these seasonal care instructions. With the right maintenance, bonsai trees may be transformed into year-round sources of delight and beauty.

Pruning and shaping techniques for different tree species

Fundamental bonsai cultivation methods such as pruning and shaping enable enthusiasts to produce and preserve the desired shape and aesthetic appeal of their bonsai trees. Different tree species, however, have distinctive growth patterns, characteristics, and needs, necessitating the use of particular pruning and shaping techniques. This section will examine pruning and shaping methods for various tree species that are frequently used in bonsai, offering details on their growth patterns and general guidelines for getting the best results. Bonsai enthusiasts can safely employ appropriate strategies to improve the beauty and artistic expression of their bonsai creations by understanding the particular requirements of various tree species.

Known for their colorful foliage and yearly leaf-shedding, deciduous trees present special opportunities for bonsai enthusiasts to display their beauty. Techniques for shaping and pruning deciduous tree species include clip-and-grow, structural pruning, and ramification pruning.

Prior to bud break, structural trimming is done during the dormant season, usually in late winter or early spring. It entails cutting back on unwanted branches, branches that are developing in unwelcome directions, and any branches that are crossing or rubbing. This pruning builds the fundamental framework and improves the overall shape of the tree.

Ramification pruning aims to increase the density of the tree and encourage secondary branching. In order to promote the formation of more delicate twigs and branches, it entails deliberately cutting back new growth to a targeted bud or leaf node. After the initial burst of spring growth, ramification pruning is often done in the growing season.

For species of coarse-leaved deciduous trees, like maples and elms, the clip-and-grow method is especially useful. A branch is permitted to grow unrestrictedly before being pruned back to promote back budding and the growth of smaller, more compact leaf pads.

Coniferous trees, which are distinguished by their scale- or needle-like foliage, offer particular difficulties and potential for bonsai enthusiasts. Coniferous tree species can be pruned and shaped using wire, pinching, and candle pruning.

The main purpose of the candle pruning technique is to shape and improve the branching structure of coniferous species, such as pine and spruce. It entails cutting back on the lengthening shoot (candle) during the spring growth season in order to focus energy on lateral buds and promote denser branching.

Using fingers or bonsai scissors, pinching entails cutting off the terminal buds or tender new growth. This method encourages back budding and encourages compactness, which aids in controlling the development and shape of coniferous trees. When fresh shoots have hardened off throughout the growing season, pinching is often done.

Coniferous trees require the use of wiring to position and shape the branches. But caution is required because coniferous trees have sensitive branches that are easily broken. Apply flexible copper or aluminum wires with caution to prevent squeezing the branches.

Flowering tree species, known for their exquisite blossoms, give bonsai presentations an enchanting quality. Techniques for shaping and pruning flowering tree species include thinning, wiring, and pruning after flowering.

Pruning flowering trees like azaleas and cherry blossoms after flowering is essential. To enable the tree to utilize the energy generated by the blooms and promote rapid growth for the upcoming season, it should be done as soon as possible after flowering.

In order to improve the tree's general structure, encourage better light penetration, and highlight the beauty of the blooms, thinning entails the selective removal of branches or foliage. Precision should be used during thining, keeping in mind the tree's natural growth pattern and aesthetic goals.

In flowering bonsai trees, wiring can be used to position and shape the branches. However, due to the fragility of some flowering tree species' branches, care must be taken to prevent damage. Be cautious of the fragile nature of the branches and use more delicate wiring techniques.

With their year-round foliage, evergreen trees give bonsai displays a sense of endurance and permanence. Techniques for pruning and shaping evergreen tree species include pinching and pruning, reducing the number of needles, and carefully placing branches.

To regulate growth and preserve the intended shape of evergreen trees, pruning and pinching are done during the growing season. Pruning improves the overall form and balance, while pinching promotes back budding and foliage density.

For evergreen coniferous species like junipers and pines, needle reduction is a technique used. It entails carefully choosing which needles to remove or shorten in order to get a more refined and compact appearance.

When shaping and positioning branches in evergreen bonsai trees, branch placement is essential. By positioning branches in a way that compliments the tree's overall form and structure, you may achieve a sense of balance and harmony while still respecting the tree's natural development pattern.

With their rich foliage and capacity to thrive indoors, tropical tree species provide bonsai enthusiasts with a distinctive experience.

Regular pruning, defoliation, and air layering are among the procedures used in shaping and pruning tropical tree species.

Due to their aggressive growth tendencies, tropical plants require regular pruning. It supports compactness, improves ramification, and growth control. To preserve the proper shape and avoid excessive elongation, regular trimming should be done.

On certain tropical tree species, defoliation, or the full removal of leaves, can be employed to promote new growth and improve branch structure. To preserve the health and vitality of the tree, this procedure should be used with care.

A technique called air layering is used to propagate existing tropical specimens into new bonsai plants. A distinct plant can be formed by stimulating root growth on a portion of a branch or trunk, enabling the construction of new bonsai with the desired characteristics.

In conclusion, bonsai artists rely heavily on pruning and shaping techniques to mold and perfect the appearance of their trees. Depending on their growth habits, characteristics, and aesthetic objectives, various tree species necessitate particular pruning and shaping techniques. Bonsai enthusiasts may create living pieces of art that perfectly capture the spirit of nature in miniature by using the right techniques, such as structural pruning, candle pruning, pinching, wiring, and selective defoliation. The artistry of bonsai can be achieved to astonishing effect through commitment, practice, and a thorough understanding of pruning and shaping procedures.

Wiring and repositioning branches

The ancient practice of cultivating miniature trees known as bonsai manages to distill the peace and beauty of nature into a tiny, delicate shape. Wiring and branch repositioning are two essential methods used by bonsai enthusiasts to mold and shape their trees into pieces of art. The grace and harmony of real trees can be captured in stunning compositions using these approaches, which enable precise manipulation and artistic expression. The goal, methods, and effects they have on the overall aesthetic appeal of bonsai trees will all be covered in this section as we examine the art and science of wiring and repositioning branches in bonsai trees.

In bonsai, wiring is a method used to direct branch growth and shape. Its main objective is to provide bonsai artists flexibility and control over the location and movement of branches so they may create compositions that are aesthetically pleasing. The following characteristics reveal the importance of wiring:

Bonsai artists can achieve exact branch placement by expertly wrapping wires around branches, assuring the appropriate structure and balance in the tree's design. This method enables the production of aesthetically beautiful compositions that are harmonious.

Bonsai enthusiasts can add dynamic movement and flow to a tree's design by using wire. Artists may give bonsai a sense of energy and vigor by subtly bending and shaping branches to mimic the way that they naturally sway and curve in the wind.

The growth of secondary branches, also known as ramification, is encouraged by properly wired branches, which gives the tree's foliage more depth and fullness. The delicate twigs and dense foliage of mature trees can be more accurately portrayed by bonsai artists by controlling the growth through wire.

Wiring has a lot of creative potential, but it's important to use the right methods and take the right precautions to protect the tree and maintain its health and vitality. The following are important rules to remember when using bonsai wiring techniques:

The right wire gauge must be selected for efficient wiring. Wire made of aluminum or copper is frequently used in bonsai because it is versatile and simple to utilize. To make sure it offers sufficient support without slicing into the bark, the wire's thickness should be proportional to the thickness of the branch.

When implementing wiring procedures, timing is crucial. During their dormant stage in late winter or early spring, when the branches are more malleable, deciduous trees are often wired. When the branches have hardened off during the growing season, evergreen trees can be wired.

Start by making a few basic loops in the wire to firmly anchor it to the branch or the trunk. Maintain a consistent space between each loop as you gradually spiral the wire around the branch. Avoid wrapping the wire too tightly to avoid damaging the branch and impeding the flow of water and nutrients.

Wired branches should receive additional support to prevent excessive bending or breakage. To spread the wire's pressure more evenly and shield the branch from any harm, wooden splints or raffia can be employed.

Wired branches need to be checked frequently to make sure they are not constricting or expanding in the wrong directions. To accommodate the tree's growth and avoid wire bite, which happens when the wire cuts into the bark, adjust the wire as needed.

Repositioning branches is yet another essential bonsai cultivation method. In order to obtain a more natural and attractive form, branches are gently bent and adjusted. When repositioning branches, the following factors and methods should be taken into account:

It's important to study and understand the growth patterns of the particular tree species before moving branches. The angles at which the branches emerge from the trunk and overall shape vary depending on the species. This comprehension will direct the repositioning procedure and guarantee a realistic and appealing end product.

Repositioning should be done carefully and gradually to prevent breaking or damaging the branches. The tree will gradually adapt to its new position if you bend the branches just a little bit at a time. Extreme or abrupt bending might result in tension and possible damage.

In bonsai design, achieving a sense of balance is essential. Consider the apparent weight and distribution of foliage while relocating branches. Make sure that there aren't too many branches on one side, which would look out of balance. Negative space, or the spaces between branches, can be used to add aesthetic interest and balance to the entire composition.

Maintaining the tree's natural shape is crucial while repositioning branches. Excessive manipulation that can appear forced or unnatural should be avoided. The objective is to highlight the tree's natural beauty while producing a unified and balanced design.

The tree needs to be properly cared for after wiring and repositioning branches in order for it to stay healthy and recover from the stress of manipulation. The following aftercare procedures ought to be followed:

Keep a vigilant eye out for any indications of wire bite, constriction, or potential harm on the wired branches. If necessary, the wire can be adjusted or removed to protect the branch.

Maintain a consistent watering plan to make sure the tree gets enough water without being waterlogged. Utilize proper fertilization techniques to supply the tree with the nutrients it needs to develop and heal.

Additional training can be needed as the bonsai tree develops to keep the desired shape and form. To perfect the design and allow for the tree's growth, regular pruning and occasional rewiring may be required.

In conclusion, wiring and branch repositioning are essential bonsai cultivation techniques that enable enthusiasts to sculpt their trees into living works of art. Artists who work with bonsai can create compositions with movement, balance, and artistic harmony by applying wires with care and gently bending them. Bonsai enthusiasts can unleash their creative potential and produce attractive bonsai trees that capture the beauty and serenity of nature in miniature by knowing the purpose, techniques, and considerations involved in wiring and repositioning. These methods not only improve bonsai's aesthetic expression but also strengthen the bond between the creator and the tree, establishing a deep appreciation for the craftsmanship and enduring beauty of bonsai.

Maintaining the health and vigor of your bonsai

The practice of bonsai, or growing miniature trees, calls for meticulous care to preserve the vitality and health of these living works of art. As bonsai enthusiasts, it is our privilege and duty to care for these miniature trees and make sure they live a long time. In this section, we'll discuss the crucial elements of keeping bonsai healthy and vigorous, such as correct maintenance, disease prevention, and methods to encourage growth and vitality.

Depending on the species, bonsai trees require different amounts of light. It's important to know your bonsai's ideal lighting setup—full sun, moderate shade, or complete shade—for its health and development. You can avoid problems like sunburn or weak growth by positioning your bonsai in accordance with its light requirements.

The health of bonsai trees depends on proper irrigation. Depending on several elements such the species, pot size, soil composition, and environmental circumstances, different amounts and frequencies of watering are needed. Root rot or dehydration can result from either overwatering or underwatering, respectively. Creating a watering schedule based on your bonsai's requirements will encourage healthy growth.

Different tree species prefer different ranges of humidity and temperature. You can create the optimal environment for your bonsai species by being aware of their unique needs. Your bonsai will be healthy and vigorous if you provide it with the proper temperature ranges and humidity levels.

Bonsai trees need soil that drains quickly and balances water retention and aeration. A good soil mixture includes organic materials, inorganic particles, and soil conditioners like perlite or vermiculite. For the overall health and vitality of your bonsai species, selecting the proper soil composition is essential.

Due to their limited root systems, bonsai plants may eventually run out of nutrients. For optimal growth and to restore vital minerals, regular fertilization is important. Its overall health and vigor will be supported by knowing the nutrient requirements of your bonsai species and utilizing the proper fertilizers.

Correct fertilizer application enables efficient nutrient uptake and guards against root burn. In the cultivation of bonsai, methods including top-dressing, liquid fertilization, and slow-release pellets are frequently used. Your bonsai will stay healthy and vigorous if fertilizers are applied at the right time and in the right amount.

In bonsai horticulture, pruning is a crucial technique that keeps the tree's health, form, and aesthetic appeal. Regular pruning encourages healthy branch structure, refocuses energy where it is most needed, and improves ramification. Your bonsai's health is ensured by knowing the fundamentals of pruning, including branch selection, timing, and procedures.

Defoliation is a method used to control bonsai trees' development, encourage ramification, and lower the size of their leaves. It entails removing some or all of the leaves at particular times of the year. When using defoliation techniques, it is crucial to use the right timing, in accordance with the species' development cycle, and to pay close attention to the health of the tree.

Maintaining the health of your bonsai requires constant vigilance in the prevention of pests and diseases. It is possible to spot pests and illnesses early by routinely checking your trees for symptoms, such as unusual leaf color, insect activity, or fungal development. Pest and disease risks can be reduced by putting preventative measures in place, such as maintaining good hygiene habits and creating ideal growing conditions.

It becomes vital to use the right control methods if pests or diseases appear. Neem oil and insecticidal soaps are examples of natural therapies that can be used to control pests. Chemical therapies may be necessary in extreme circumstances. To prevent damaging the tree or the surrounding area, vigilance should be taken.

Repotting is a crucial part of bonsai maintenance since it guarantees the root system's health and avoids root congestion. Based on its rate of growth and root development, each bonsai species has a unique repotting plan. To reduce stress and encourage healthy root growth, repotting should be done when the tree is dormant and using the right methods.

Root pruning is done during repotting to keep the relationship between the tree's foliage and root system balanced. The act of root pruning promotes the growth of new roots and aids in the removal of circling or old roots. Your bonsai will be healthier and more vigorous overall if you pay close attention to root pruning techniques and follow the right maintenance procedures.

Maintaining bonsai health requires modifying care procedures in accordance with the changing patterns of the seasons. The survival of cold-sensitive species is ensured through winter protection, such as frost shelter or adequate insulation. To prevent dehydration, summertime care may entail more shading or watering. It will be beneficial for your bonsai's overall health if you modify your care procedures to meet its seasonal needs.

To avoid problems like fungal diseases, your bonsai has to have adequate air circulation. Bonsai should be placed in well-ventilated spaces, and overcrowding should be avoided. Additionally, maintaining appropriate air quality will enhance the health and vitality of the trees by keeping them away from contaminants or hazardous gasses.

Finally, preserving the vitality and health of bonsai is a rewarding job that requires expertise, consideration, and close attention to detail. Bonsai enthusiasts can assure the longevity and beauty of their miniature trees by understanding the special requirements of bonsai, using appropriate watering and fertilizing methods, practicing pruning and defoliation, managing pests and diseases, and taking environmental considerations into account. In addition to investing in their well-being, preserving the health and vitality of bonsai is also an expression of our admiration for the beauty and harmony of nature in its miniature form.

CHAPTER
V
Advanced Techniques and Styling

Advanced bonsai techniques: grafting and air-layering

The ancient practice of growing miniature trees known as bonsai offers enthusiasts a wide range of ways to experiment with. Advanced methods like grafting and air-layering enable bonsai artists to push the boundaries of creativity and refine their aesthetic vision. These methods go beyond fundamental procedures like pruning and wiring. In this section, grafting and air-layering will be the main topics of discussion as we delve into the complex world of advanced bonsai techniques. We will investigate the fundamentals, processes, and advantages of these techniques, providing insights into their application as well as the reshaping effects that they are capable of having on bonsai.

Grafting is a process that combines two different plant parts to create a single, cohesive whole. Grafting is a technique used in bonsai to add new branches, alter the direction of growth, or give a tree desirable traits. Successful grafting relies heavily on the compatibility, time, and method elements.

Approach grafting, thread grafting, and side-veneer grafting are only a few of the grafting techniques used in bonsai horticulture. Each technique entails particular considerations and measures to guarantee correct alignment, nutrient flow, and healing.

Grafting has many advantages for bonsai artists. The introduction of branches from several species or cultivars is made possible, resulting in the development of new leaves, flower hues, or growth patterns. Intricate branch structures can be developed more easily through grafting, which encourages ramification and aesthetic refinement.

Precision, perseverance, and knowledge of the species' development traits are all necessary for successful grafting. There could be difficulties, like incompatibilities, graft rejection, or the requirement for continuing maintenance. However, with careful preparation and execution, grafting can produce outstanding outcomes.

The process of "air-layering" promotes the development of new roots on a chosen branch while it is still connected to the parent tree. Bypassing seed germination and conventional propagation methods, this technology enables the development of new individual trees from pre-existing branches.

On a chosen branch, a partial incision or ring of bark removal are required for air-layering. New roots are encouraged to sprout in the exposed area by this technique. Once roots have formed, it is possible to cut the branch away from the parent tree to make a standalone bonsai specimen.

With the aid of air-layering, bonsai masters can produce new trees with the desired traits. It enables the preservation of rare cultivars as well as the propagation of species that are challenging to root. Air-layering also produces specimens with established root systems, which hastens the growth of mature trees.

Timing, appropriate wound care, and sufficient moisture levels are essential for effective air-layering. Certain methods, including employing hormones to encourage root growth or installing misting systems, can improve success rates. Aesthetic harmony is further ensured by choosing the proper branch and taking into account the bonsai's overall design.

In bonsai, grafting and air-layering open up new avenues for aesthetic expression. By combining traits from various trees, these techniques enable the creation of distinctive compositions and the miniature representation of nature. Innovation and creativity have limitless potential.

Bonsai artists can revive older or less appealing trees using modern techniques. Artists can give old specimens new life by grafting or air-layering new branches or root systems, transforming them into intriguing and dynamic bonsai creations.

Air-layering and grafting both promote experimentation and the study of hybridization. By fusing multiple species or introducing features that were previously absent in a given species, artists can push the limits of traditional bonsai.

Advanced bonsai techniques take commitment, effort, and ongoing education to master. As grafting and air-layering techniques are more understood by bonsai artists, their skill set grows, allowing them to take on new tasks and produce bonsai of unparalleled beauty.

In conclusion, air-layering and grafting are two advanced bonsai techniques that provide limitless opportunities for horticultural research and creative expression. These methods give bonsai artists the tools they need to shape and transform trees, fusing various species, adding new branches, and establishing whole new starts. Bonsai enthusiasts embark on a voyage of expertise, experimentation, and ongoing learning as they delve into the worlds of grafting and air-layering. These advanced techniques enable bonsai artists to stretch the limits of their imagination and produce breath-taking outcomes, further enhancing the alluring bonsai art form.

Creating different bonsai styles: formal, informal, cascade, etc.

The ancient practice of cultivating miniature trees known as bonsai allows an infinite range of aesthetic expression. The capacity to develop several bonsai styles is one of the main features that draws bonsai enthusiasts. Artists can shape and design their trees in a variety of styles, from formal and symmetrical to casual and cascading, to transmit particular aesthetics and elicit particular feelings. The various bonsai styles will be explored in this section, and the principles, characteristics, and methods used to produce each style will be looked at. Bonsai artists may release their creativity and create magnificent miniature works of art by grasping the fundamentals of each style.

The formal bonsai method, sometimes referred to as "Chokkan" in Japanese, places emphasis on a symmetrical and balanced arrangement. The trunk of the tree is straight and upright, while the branches are well organized. Formal bonsai frequently emanate a sense of calmness and peace that is reminiscent of the aesthetics of traditional Japanese gardens.

A dominating central trunk with carefully chosen primary, secondary, and tertiary branches that taper from base to apex is one of the formal style's key design components. The branches' equal spacing and perfect balance represent the elegance and understatement that define this design.

Pruning, wiring, and shaping must be done with great care to retain the necessary symmetry and structure when creating a formal bonsai style. The formal style's grace and refinement must be maintained regularly by careful branch selection and attentive attention to detail.

The informal bonsai style, sometimes referred to as "Moyogi" in Japanese, aims to imitate nature's asymmetrical and natural beauty. This design approach celebrates irregularity and nature, capturing the character of a tree's natural growth. Informal bonsai convey a feeling of motion, freedom, and harmony with nature.

Informal bonsai have a trunk line that is uneven and frequently has bends, twists, and soft curves. The branches' radial growth gives the appearance of dynamic movement in all directions. The asymmetrical placement of the branches and foliage perfectly captures the natural irregularity.

A natural and harmonious appearance can be achieved by carefully pruning, wiring, and positioning an informal bonsai. Using methods such as directional pruning and selective wiring, an emphasis is placed on the creation of realistic branch structures in the tree. Balanced foliage density and the encouragement of natural growth patterns are two aspects of routine care.

The cascade bonsai style, also known as "Kengai" in Japanese, conveys drama, elegance, and a sense of motion. This design imitates the downward-cascading trunk of a tree growing on a steep mountainside, which frequently extends below the base of the pot.

Cascade bonsai have a prominent trunk that protrudes past the rim of the pot and displays a downward curve or cascade. The upward growth of the branches and foliage balances the downward flow of the stem. This aesthetic produces a strong visual impression and a sense of drama.

To achieve the correct curve and balance when building a cascade bonsai, careful branch selection and wiring are necessary. In order to maintain the expanded portion of the tree, sufficient soil anchorage is required, as well as managing the weight and balance of the cascading stem.

The Japanese term "Bunjin" for the literati bonsai style also refers to a sense of grace, uniqueness, and aesthetic expression. This artistic movement, which draws its inspiration from literati poetry and painting, honors unique and unconventional tree forms, frequently characterized by slender, twisted trunks and sparse foliage.

Literati bonsai have long, slender trunks that bend and turn, giving them a sense of age and character. With foliage clusters put in appropriate locations to improve the overall beauty, the branches are sparsely and carefully organized. This style places an emphasis on whimsy, abstract thinking, and elegance all at the same time.

Careful wiring and pruning are required while shaping a literati bonsai in order to get the desired slender and irregular trunk shape. To highlight the distinctive nature of the tree, strategies including defoliation and selective branch removal are used. To preserve the grace and uniqueness of the literati style, routine maintenance requires careful monitoring of branch development and foliage placement.

The semi-cascade form has a trunk that partially extends from the pot's base, giving the appearance of a cascading effect. This style exhibits a balanced and pleasing design by fusing aspects of the cascade and casual styles.

The goal of the windswept style is to depict how a tree grows as a result of high winds. It displays resilience and adaptation to difficult circumstances with its tilted stem and branches that seem to be swept in one direction.

In a single bonsai composition, many trunks are grown in the multi-trunk style. The interconnection of trees in a forest or grove is represented by this style, which gives the impression of unity and natural harmony.

In conclusion, developing various bonsai styles is an exciting adventure that enables bonsai artists to connect with the essence of nature and express their artistic vision. Each bonsai style conveys a different aesthetic, from the chokkan style's formal, symmetrical elegance to the moyogi style's organic, free-spirited beauty. The creative potential of bonsai enthusiasts can be unlocked by learning the principles, design aspects, and techniques unique to each style, allowing them to produce magnificent tiny works of art that captivate and inspire viewers. The universe of bonsai styles invites artists to begin on a lifetime path of growth, discovery, and aesthetic mastery by providing limitless opportunities for artistic inquiry and self-expression.

Accent plants and display considerations

The craftsmanship in the captivating realm of bonsai goes beyond the miniature trees themselves. Accent plants, sometimes referred to as companion plants or kusamono, are essential for generating aesthetically pleasing compositions and boosting the overall visual impact of bonsai displays. These carefully chosen plants, which frequently have a variety of leaf colors, textures, and blooming patterns, provide the bonsai arrangement depth, balance, and visual interest. In this section, we'll dig into the fascinating world of bonsai accent plants and examine the factors that go into designing jaw-dropping displays. Bonsai enthusiasts can improve their artistic expression and produce engaging compositions that genuinely come alive by comprehending the value of accent plants and the fundamentals of display design.

Accent plants are chosen as a visual partner that harmonizes with the bonsai tree's characteristics, complementing and enhancing the bonsai tree. They offer a background of color, texture, and form, emphasizing the bonsai's central feature and forming a unified and aesthetically pleasing presentation.

Accent plants contribute to the bonsai display's sense of size and context, giving the impression of a natural setting. The natural environment of the tree can be accurately recreated in a miniature setting by bonsai artists by carefully choosing plants that are native to that environment or have similar growth requirements.

Accent plants offer seasonal appeal, which adds to the ever-changing beauty of bonsai displays. These plants contribute a dynamic aspect that varies throughout the year, providing a visual journey and capturing the essence of nature's cycles, whether through vibrant blooms, colorful foliage, or distinctive textures.

The unique characteristics of the bonsai tree should be taken into account while choosing accent plants. The accent plant's size, shape, leaves color, and general design should match the tree's. It should accentuate the bonsai's aesthetic impact without overpowering or competing for attention.

Accent plants provide you the chance to showcase a wide variety of foliage types, textures, and forms. The accent plant should give a pleasing contrast or compliment the leaves of the bonsai tree, adding depth and visual appeal to the design. It can range from delicate ferns and grasses to bold-leaved plants or those with intriguing patterns.

To ensure year-round interest in the bonsai display, it is essential to take the accent plant's seasonal qualities into account. A pleasing fusion of components that captivate spectators all year long can be achieved by choosing plants with blossoms, shifting foliage colors, or distinctive features throughout the seasons.

A visually appealing presentation depends on the accent plant and bonsai tree being in proportional harmony with one another. A sense of balance and cohesiveness should be achieved within the composition by matching the size, height, and growth pattern of the accent plant with the bonsai tree's size and style.

The accent plant and bonsai's container or pot are crucial components of the entire display. The accent plant should be placed in a container that complements the bonsai tree's design and aesthetic while highlighting its distinctive traits. To establish a harmonic composition, the color, kind of material, and shape of the container should all be carefully examined.

To achieve balance and harmony in the presentation, the accent plant's placement in relation to the bonsai tree is crucial. The accent plant should be placed to draw in the viewer's eye, create a sense of movement and unity between the two pieces, and take into account the visual flow.

Carefully analyze the spatial interactions between the bonsai tree, accent plant, and other display pieces like pebbles or figurines. The composition's negative space or empty spaces can be employed to emphasize the composition's key parts and foster a sense of calm.

Displays of bonsai can have symbolic or cultural significance. Accent plants can be chosen based on historical symbolism or personal meaning, giving the composition's overall depth and narrative a new dimension.

Accent plants may demand different amounts of water and nutrients than a bonsai tree. To ensure the accent plant's health and vigor, careful consideration should be made to watering and fertilizing it. It may be required to modify fertilizing and watering regimens in order to accommodate each plant's unique requirements.

Accent plants must be regularly pruned and groomed to keep their size, form, and general beauty. To regulate growth, encourage branching, and maintain the intended form of the accent plant, pruning techniques like pinching, trimming, or selective pruning can be used.

Accent plants, like bonsai trees, may need varying maintenance depending on the season. To guarantee the health and lifespan of the accent plant, necessary protection from frost or other extreme weather should be taken into account, along with suitable adjustments to lighting and temperature.

In conclusion, accent plants are essential for bonsai presentations because they give compositions depth, balance, and aesthetic intrigue. These specifically chosen plants not only go well with the bonsai tree, but they also add to the overall aesthetic impact and combine the elements in a pleasing way. Bonsai enthusiasts may create compelling displays that change throughout the year by taking into account the qualities of the bonsai tree, choosing accent plants with varied foliage, textures, and forms, and paying attention to seasonal variations. The development of harmonic compositions that captivate viewers and communicate compelling visual stories also depends on careful consideration of container placement, selection, and spatial relationships. Accent plants enhance the aesthetic of the small landscape in bonsai exhibits, highlighting nature's beauty in miniature, and inspiring visitors to delve deeper into the fascinating world of bonsai.

Exhibiting and participating in bonsai shows

The artistry, expertise, and commitment of bonsai enthusiasts are joyfully celebrated at bonsai shows. These gatherings unite a community of bonsai creators, collectors, and admirers to exhibit their miniature masterpieces, share knowledge, and appreciate the beauty of these living sculptures. The world of exhibiting and taking part in bonsai exhibits will be examined in this section, from the planning and selecting stages through the rewarding experience of introducing bonsai to a larger audience. Bonsai artists can improve their abilities, get insightful feedback, and support the expansion of the bonsai community by realizing the importance of bonsai shows and seizing the chance to exhibit.

The art of bonsai is promoted and its cultural and artistic value is made more widely known through bonsai shows. By displaying their trees, artists help to preserve and spread bonsai as a living art form, encouraging others to admire it and continue their own artistic endeavors.

A special opportunity for bonsai artists to impart their expertise, methods, and experiences to other enthusiasts is presented through bonsai shows. Artists can motivate and instruct others through demonstrations, workshops, and discussions, establishing a culture of cooperation and expansion within the bonsai community.

Participating in bonsai competitions forces artists to hone their craft and pursue excellence. An artist's skill and aesthetics are continually challenged by the meticulous refinement, style, and attention to detail required to prepare a tree for show.

An important part of the preparation process is picking the ideal tree for display. Considerations should be made for elements including tree species, health, maturity, and aesthetic appeal. For exhibition, trees with extraordinary qualities, distinctive traits, and well-developed ramification are frequently desired.

Artists spend a lot of time and effort perfecting the tree's form, balance, and overall appearance before the performance. Wiring, pruning, and selective defoliation are among of the methods used to accentuate the tree's inherent beauty and produce a captivating composition.

It is crucial to choose a pot that matches the tree's size and design. The selection of the display stand or table, as well as the positioning of accent plants, moss, and other ornamental components that improve the overall appearance, should also be taken into consideration.

The exhibition space's tree placement must be carefully planned out in order to maintain coherence, balance, and visual flow. The placement of trees should emphasize their greatest qualities and result in a harmonic composition that is pleasing to the eye.

Experienced bonsai masters judge the displayed trees at bonsai exhibits frequently using criteria including trunk movement, branch structure, overall health, and aesthetics. Judges' comments offer insightful feedback that helps artists in honing their skills and aesthetic vision.

The chance to interact with other bonsai enthusiasts, collectors, and professionals is priceless during bonsai exhibits. Conversations, ideas sharing, and the development of deep connections among artists can promote a spirit of camaraderie and support for one another.

For artists, taking part in bonsai displays is a transforming event that fosters personal growth. The process of getting ready for a display forces artists to hone their skills, expand their knowledge of bonsai aesthetics, and push the limits of their imagination.

Participating in bonsai events enables artists to encourage and uplift others, particularly those who are new to the art form. Artists can inspire others to start their own bonsai adventures by displaying their bonsai trees and sharing their journey.

Bonsai competitions offer a chance to support the expansion and improvement of the bonsai community. Artists can support the next generation of bonsai enthusiasts by volunteering, hosting workshops or lectures, or providing their knowledge in a variety of other ways.

In conclusion, showing at and taking part in bonsai events are wonderful activities that honor the talent, commitment, and enthusiasm of bonsai artists. These gatherings generate a sense of community, information sharing, and individual development in addition to promoting the bonsai art. Artists contribute to the expansion of the bonsai community by diligently preparing their trees, accepting the judging procedure, and interacting with other enthusiasts. They also serve as an inspiration for others to pursue their own artistic endeavors. Bonsai shows are effective venues for showcasing the beauty of these living sculptures, inspiring others, and recognizing the captivating art form that is bonsai.

CHAPTER VI
Troubleshooting
and Problem-Solving

Common issues faced by beginners and their solutions

Starting a bonsai cultivation adventure can be thrilling and difficult, especially for novices. Newcomers frequently run into recurring problems as they explore the world of bonsai, which might impede their development and confidence. These difficulties may be overcome, though, with the right instruction and comprehension, helping beginners to succeed in their bonsai pursuits. In this section, we'll look at some frequent problems new bonsai growers encounter and offer practical solutions to help them overcome these difficulties. Beginners can build a solid foundation and have a fulfilling bonsai experience by tackling these difficulties head-on.

One of the primary challenges for newcomers to bonsai cultivation is their lack of information and experience. Fundamental ideas like tree species selection, care procedures, and styling principles could be difficult for them to comprehend.

Beginners should take the time to study about bonsai from a variety of sources in order to get past this problem. Books, online courses, workshops, and local bonsai organizations all offer helpful advice. Getting involved with seasoned bonsai enthusiasts and looking for mentorship can both greatly speed up learning.

Beginners frequently struggle to comprehend the precise care requirements for bonsai trees, such as watering, fertilizing, and insect control. Unreliable maintenance procedures can cause stress in trees, poor development, and even death.

It's critical for newcomers to educate themselves on the precise maintenance requirements of the tree species they have chosen. They can give the tree the best care by learning about its natural environment, preferred climate, and seasonal needs. The well-being of the tree will be guaranteed by routinely monitoring its health and modifying care procedures accordingly.

Beginners could find it difficult to use the right pruning and shaping procedures, which frequently leads to incorrect branch placement, imbalanced designs, and damaged tree health.

Beginners should learn and put into practice the basic concepts of shaping and pruning in order to resolve this issue. Beginners can create balanced and aesthetically beautiful patterns by learning about the precise processes, such as directed pruning, branch selection, and ramification development. Attending pruning classes and asking advice from seasoned bonsai growers can both be excellent ways to get practical skills.

For beginners, finding the ideal watering balance can be difficult. Underwatering can result in dehydration and tree stress, while overwatering can result in root rot and other illnesses.

By analyzing the soil moisture levels, learning the particular watering requirements of their tree species, and modifying watering frequency as necessary, beginners can learn to comprehend the water demands of their bonsai trees. The ideal moisture balance can be maintained by using well-draining bonsai soil and using suitable watering methods, such as watering until the bottom of the pot.

Beginners may struggle to recognize and control illnesses and pests that damage bonsai trees. Delay in diagnosis and treatment can cause serious harm to trees, including their eventual death.

Learning about typical pests and illnesses that damage bonsai trees is crucial for novices. Pest and disease problems can be reduced through frequent inspections, early diagnosis, and prompt management using organic or chemical treatments. Effective pest and disease management can be aided by consulting with local gardening professionals or seeking the counsel of experienced bonsai growers.

Beginners might find it difficult to comprehend the seasonal care adjustments needed for bonsai trees. Negative effects on the health and growth of trees might result from failing to adjust care procedures to seasonal variations.

Beginners should familiarize themselves with the particular seasonal maintenance requirements of their tree species. They will be able to modify watering, fertilizing, and weather protection as necessary if they are aware of how temperature, humidity, light levels, and dormancy affect bonsai trees.

Bonsai maintenance needs patience because trees grow and change over a long period of time. Beginners could lose motivation or interest if they don't get results right away or run into obstacles along the way.

For beginners to bonsai, developing patience and adopting a long-term viewpoint are essential. Beginners will learn to appreciate the development of trees by understanding that bonsai is a journey that lasts for years or even decades. Beginners will stay motivated and dedicated by establishing reasonable goals, acknowledging little accomplishments, and finding enjoyment in the routine maintenance of bonsai trees.

In conclusion, although beginners to bonsai horticulture may encounter typical difficulties, these problems may be solved with information, practice, and an eagerness to learn. Beginners can provide a strong foundation for their bonsai journey by addressing gaps in knowledge, tree care, trimming procedures, watering, pest and disease management, seasonal adjustments, and learning patience. Beginners can effectively traverse these difficulties by seeking advice from seasoned practitioners, interacting with the bonsai community, and embracing the process of constant learning. Beginners who are persistent and dedicated to studying can grow healthy bonsai trees and enjoy the pleasures and rewards of this age-old art.

Recognizing and addressing bonsai health problems

Bonsai tree cultivation calls much more than simply creative vision and expert technique. Additionally, it necessitates having a sharp eye for spotting and resolving any potential health issues. Since bonsai are living things, they may have a range of problems with pests, illnesses, nutritional shortages, and environmental stress. In order to maintain the long-term vitality and well-being of bonsai trees, it is crucial to identify these health issues and discuss practical solutions in this section.

The first step in keeping bonsai plants healthy is to observe them carefully. Observing the tree's foliage, branches, and overall appearance frequently enables bonsai enthusiasts to see potential problems before they become serious. There may be a problem if there are signs like yellowing leaves, wilting, discoloration, abnormal growth patterns, or the presence of pests. By keeping a close eye on the bonsai's health, potential problems can be addressed quickly and prevented from getting worse.

The health of bonsai trees is seriously threatened by pests and diseases. Aphids, scale insects, mites, and caterpillars are typical pests, and bacterial, viral, and fungal pathogens can cause illnesses. Distorted leaves, webbing, discoloration, or abnormal growth patterns are a few indicators of a disease or pest infestation. In such circumstances, appropriate treatment methods may be used, such as the use of natural pesticides, the application of fungicides, or the adoption of cultural norms like increasing air circulation and upholding hygienic standards.

Bonsai plants' development and health can be hindered by nutrient deficiencies. Stunted growth, yellowing or browning leaves, and overall poor health are common indicators of nutritional deficiency. In order to solve these deficiencies, it is essential to understand the particular nutrient needs of the different tree species. Organic or synthetic fertilization can supply the essential nutrients that the soil is lacking. The right pH levels and watering procedures are also important for nutrient uptake and overall tree health.

Due to their sensitivity to the environment, bonsai trees can suffer greatly from stresses like high heat, poor lighting, inadequate watering, or insufficient humidity. Environmental stress can be identified by looking for wilted leaves, leaf burn, or an overall loss in the tree's vigor. It's important to offer ideal microclimates, optimal lighting conditions, consistent watering schedules, and optimum ventilation in order to handle these problems. Stress is reduced and the resilience and overall health of the bonsai are ensured by creating a pleasant habitat.

Wiring and pruning are crucial bonsai cultivation procedures, but they must be done carefully to prevent harming the tree's health. An excessive amount of stress and exposed wounds caused by improper pruning might act as entry points for diseases and pests. Similar to loose wiring, tight wiring or wiring that is left on for a long time can harm the branches and prevent a tree's normal growth. Proper pruning procedures, such as making clean cuts and encouraging balanced branch structure, should be put into practice. The health of the tree must also be maintained by keeping an eye on wired branches and cutting the wire off before it cuts the bark.

In conclusion, successful bonsai cultivation depends on identifying and resolving bonsai health issues. Bonsai enthusiasts may address problems with pests, illnesses, nutritional deficiencies, and environmental stress by keeping a close eye out for warning signs and responding as necessary. The long-term health, vitality, and visual attractiveness of these living works of art can be guaranteed by bonsai enthusiasts by recognizing the particular requirements of their bonsai trees and using practical techniques. Bonsai trees can flourish with constant monitoring and pro-active care, mesmerizing observers with their grace and enduring beauty.

Dealing with pests, diseases, and environmental challenges

The cultivation of bonsai is a delicate and complex art form that needs careful consideration and care. Bonsai enthusiasts frequently run into problems including diseases, pests, and stresses from the environment while caring for these miniature trees. Maintaining the health and vigor of bonsai trees requires an understanding of effective solutions to these problems. In the context of bonsai cultivation, we will look at methods for addressing pests, diseases, and environmental issues in this section.

Bonsai trees can be severely harmed by pests, which can cause damage to the leaves, stems, and roots of the trees. Insects including aphids, scale insects, mites, and caterpillars are frequent pests in bonsai growth. Identification of the exact pest species infesting the tree is the first stage in dealing with pests. Pests or their obvious symptoms, like sticky buildup or webbing, can be found by carefully examining the foliage, stems, and undersides of leaves.

Once the pest has been located, appropriate prevention measures can be put in place. In order to have as little of an environmental impact as possible, organic insecticides like neem oil or insecticidal soap are frequently preferred in bonsai cultivation. Additionally, some forms of infestations may respond well to physical techniques like hand-picking pests or employing water sprays. To prevent harmful insect populations from establishing and seriously harming the bonsai, regular monitoring and early management are essential.

Diseases can weaken and impede the growth and development of bonsai trees. Pathogens that cause bacterial, viral, and fungal infections are typically to blame for outbreaks of bonsai disease. Discoloration, wilting, lesions, or abnormal growth patterns on leaves, stems, or roots are signs of disease.

Implementing suitable treatment strategies requires accurate disease diagnosis. To correctly identify the pathogen, it is advised to seek the advice of specialists or study reference books designed especially for bonsai diseases. Targeted treatments, like fungicides or bactericides, can be used once the illness has been diagnosed. To prevent the illness from spreading, it may occasionally be necessary to prune the damaged portions or remove the infected plants totally.

When it comes to diseases affecting bonsai, prevention is always preferable to cure. Disinfecting tools, pots, and work surfaces can help lower the risk of spreading diseases by maintaining good hygiene standards. Additionally, it is possible to reduce the likelihood of disease formation by providing good soil drainage, allowing sufficient air circulation, and avoiding overwatering.

Because they are sensitive to environmental factors, bonsai trees might suffer from stresses like temperature extremes, inadequate lighting, inappropriate watering, or poor air circulation. The health of bonsai trees depends on recognizing and resolving these environmental issues.

Bonsai trees can become stressed by extreme temperatures, which can cause wilting, leaf burn, or even death. Temperature-related stress can be reduced by creating suitable microclimates, such as shade or shelter during hot summers or chilly winters. Similar to this, it is crucial to provide the right lighting conditions for the process of photosynthesis and the tree's overall growth, whether this comes from grow lights or natural sunlight.

It's crucial to follow proper watering procedures to keep bonsai healthy. Underwatering can result in dehydration and wilting, while overwatering can result in root rot and fungal diseases. For the proper balance to be maintained, it is essential to comprehend the watering requirements of various tree species and to monitor the soil moisture content.

For the purpose of preventing the development of fungal illnesses and encouraging healthy growth, proper air circulation is crucial. Adequate ventilation can lower the danger of fungal infections and enhance the overall air quality surrounding the bonsai, especially in humid situations.

In conclusion, managing pests, illnesses, and environmental issues is a crucial component of bonsai production. The long-term health and vitality of bonsai lovers' miniature trees can be guaranteed by being vigilant, taking quick action, and providing proactive maintenance. For bonsai health to be maintained, regular observation, accurate identification, and appropriate treatment procedures for diseases and pests are essential. The health of bonsai trees also depends on establishing ideal climatic conditions that take into account temperature extremes, appropriate lighting, proper watering, and good air circulation. Bonsai enthusiasts can overcome these difficulties and carry on appreciating the beauty and creativity of their little works of art by applying knowledge, perseverance, and dedication.

CHAPTER VII
Bonsai Beyond the Basics

Exploring advanced bonsai concepts and styles

The ancient practice of cultivating miniature trees in pots is known as bonsai, and it offers an endless opportunity for learning and discovery. As bonsai enthusiasts develop expertise and knowledge, they frequently discover that they are drawn to investigating more complex ideas and techniques. The limits of conventional bonsai are pushed by these advanced techniques and styles, which also promote more artistic expression. We shall go into the realm of advanced bonsai concepts and styles in this section, looking at the methods and concepts that take bonsai to new heights.

Yamadori is the term used to describe the process of gathering trees from their native environments, such as forests or mountains. These collected trees frequently have distinctive qualities including weathered bark, intriguing twists, and an aged appearance. To create a bonsai masterpiece with yamadori material, one needs sophisticated abilities in tree gathering, root pruning, and styling.

Grafting is a sophisticated method for joining various plant elements, including branches or roots, to a bonsai tree. By using this method, bonsai artists can add new species, change the tree's traits, or fix any damage. For successful grafting and long-term health, patience, plant physiology knowledge, and accuracy are necessary.

Without removing the tree from its roots, air layering is a technique used to grow new bonsai trees from an existing tree. Bonsai artists can produce more trees with favorable traits by making a wound on the branch and promoting the growth of new roots. To ensure the effective establishment of the new tree during air layering, competence in scheduling, wound healing, and appropriate maintenance are required.

In order to simulate the effects of aging, weathering, and natural forces, deadwood techniques entail generating or improving regions of deadwood on a bonsai tree. Jin (stripped bark) and shari (stripped trunk) techniques give the tree personality, depth, and a sense of history. To get results that look natural and are aesthetically pleasing, advanced knowledge of carving tools, techniques, and an understanding of the tree's reaction to deadwood work are required.

Literati is a highly refined and artistic bonsai style distinguished by tall, slender trunks and sparse foliage, often known as bunjin or "elegant scholar" style. The purpose of this look is to convey grace, elegance, and age. Literati bonsai frequently have complex and dramatic trunk twists, which give them a distinctive and alluring appearance.

A bonsai tree designed in the multi-trunk style has numerous trunks that grow from a single root system. This design imitates the organic growth patterns of trees observed in groves and woods. The trunks are thoughtfully placed in a pleasing composition, frequently having different heights, thicknesses, and angles. The multi-trunk design presents a chance to highlight the interaction of many trunks while generating movement and visual appeal.

Multiple bonsai trees are arranged in a single container as part of group planting, sometimes referred to as forest or landscape planting, to give the impression of a miniature forest or landscape. The choice of trees, their placement, and the aesthetic harmony they create must all be carefully considered when designing in this style. Group plantings provide a lively and expressive portrayal of the harmony and beauty of nature.

Advanced bonsai concepts also include the skill of exhibiting bonsai, which goes beyond individual trees. It is crucial to comprehend the concepts of composition, balance, and harmony when deciding where to arrange bonsai trees, accent plants, and display components. Advanced bonsai display techniques include making seasonal arrangements, adding suiseki (viewing stones), or enhancing the presentation with accessories like scroll paintings or bonsai stands.

In conclusion, learning more about advanced bonsai concepts and techniques enables bonsai enthusiasts to go beyond the bounds of conventional methods and to show their unique creativity and aesthetic vision. The use of methods like yamadori, grafting, air layering, and deadwood work allows bonsai artists to advance their craft and produce trees that are genuinely unique. Additionally, contemporary bonsai designs like literati, multi-trunk, group planting, and inventive exhibition methods provide fresh opportunities for individual expression and enjoyment of the art form. A world of limitless opportunities awaits bonsai enthusiasts as they set out on this explorational journey, where the art and beauty of bonsai continue to evolve and inspire.

Collecting and selecting bonsai material

Careful selection and collection of acceptable plant material is one of the core components of bonsai art. When buying bonsai material, it's important to take into account a number of variables, including the tree's species, size, age, and aesthetic potential. In this section, we'll discuss the value of gathering and choosing bonsai material while emphasizing the essential factors to take into account and the methods to employ when doing so.

Yamadori is the term used to describe the process of taking trees out of their natural environments, such as forests, mountains, or other types of landscapes. These gathered trees frequently have distinctive qualities including an aged appearance, worn bark, and intriguing twists. To preserve the long-term health of the gathered trees and their natural habitats, yamadori collection requires knowledge of tree species, identification, appropriate collecting procedures, and an understanding of local regulations and sustainability practices.

Plant nurseries that specialize in providing plants appropriate for bonsai are another typical source of bonsai material. Numerous species, sizes, and pre-trained bonsai specimens are available at nurseries. When choosing nursery-grown plants, it's important to look at the plant's overall health, take into account its bonsai styling potential, and make sure the tree is compatible with the area's climate and growth conditions.

Pre-bonsai material, which are young trees or shrubs with the potential to become bonsai, is frequently available in garden centers. The ability to grow and mold the tree from an early stage is offered by these plants, which are typically affordable. Pre-bonsai material selection is assessing a plant's root system, trunk, and branch structure to determine its viability for future bonsai training.

In bonsai art, the choice of tree species is vital. The growth patterns, leaf forms, bark textures, and responses to training methods vary between species. It is crucial to take into account the species' appropriateness for bonsai cultivation, its adaptability to the local temperature, and the desired aesthetic qualities while choosing bonsai material.

A bonsai tree's trunk is its support system and a key component of its overall aesthetic appeal. The thickness, taper, movement, and nebari (root flare) of the trunk should all be taken into consideration while choosing bonsai material. Bonsai can be made from trees that have distinctive trunk characteristics, such as bends, scars, or surface textures.

For a bonsai design to be balanced and harmonious, the branch structure is crucial. The overall appearance and proportion of the tree are enhanced by strategically arranged branches with good distribution and taper. Consider the potential of the current branches for future style and refining when choosing bonsai material.

The root system and the nebari, or the visible surface roots, are essential components of bonsai aesthetics. Trees with strong, radial root systems provide the composition stability and impact. To establish a strong foundation for the tree's future development, bonsai material's nebari and root structure must be evaluated.

Material for bonsai should be in good health, be free of serious diseases or pests, and exhibit strong development. Selecting plants with weak or damaged health is best avoided because they could find it difficult to survive and flourish as bonsai. During this selection phase, it is essential to look at the plant's overall health, foliage color, and lack of any serious pests or illnesses.

In conclusion, in order to grow stunning and durable bonsai trees, acquiring and choosing bonsai material is an essential first step. It is crucial to take into account the species, trunk characteristics, branch structure, nebari, and general health of the tree when gathering from natural landscapes or purchasing from nurseries and garden centers. A beautiful bonsai specimen can be created from any material, provided it has the ability to do so. Enthusiasts for bonsai go on a path of creativity, perseverance, and admiration for the natural beauty of trees in miniature form as they delve into the world of bonsai material selection.

Artistic bonsai photography and documentation

In miniature trees, the living art form of bonsai embodies the beauty and soul of nature. Artistic photography and documentation are crucial for capturing the fine intricacies of bonsai and showcasing them. It is possible to preserve, share, and appreciate the creativity and workmanship of bonsai for future generations by using expert photography techniques and careful documentation. The significance of artistic bonsai photography and documentation will be discussed in this section, along with the methods and factors to be taken into account while attempting to capture the essence of bonsai trees.

Unique characteristics of bonsai trees include interesting nebari (root flare), delicate foliage, and complicated branch structure. These aspects of the tree's beauty and personality are intended to be conveyed through artistic bonsai photography. Close-ups, imaginative angles, and depth of field are just a few of the photographic methods that photographers can use to highlight the smallest details and produce aesthetically captivating photos.

Bonsai trees are dynamic living sculptures that undergo constant modification. The artistry and craftsmanship that go into each tree can be preserved by photographing bonsai. Photographs document the tree's development, styling, and transformation and serve as a historical record. They also give enthusiasts and artists a chance to reflect on the tree's journey and the clever strategies used.

The beauty and complexity of bonsai art can be inspired by and explained to viewers through artistic bonsai photography. A fascination for this age-old art form can be sparked by beautifully caught photographs that generate feelings and draw in viewers. People can gain a deeper understanding and appreciation for bonsai as a living art form by learning about various bonsai styles, species, and cultural influences through aesthetically striking images.

The right lighting is essential for bonsai photography. Since it highlights the actual texture and color of the tree, natural light is frequently favored. For accentuating the fine details and eliminating harsh shadows, soft, diffused light is preferable. The visual impact can be improved by experimenting with various lighting situations, such as early morning or late afternoon sunlight.

The positioning and arrangement of elements within the frame is referred to as composition. Use the rule of thirds, leading lines, and negative space while taking pictures of bonsai to get a balanced and aesthetically beautiful composition. To add depth and interest to the image, play around with different angles, such as overhead photos, close-ups of the leaves, or capturing the tree in its natural setting.

By adjusting the depth of field, photographers can choose focus on particular bonsai parts. A narrow depth of field is produced by using a wide aperture (small f-number), blurring the background and emphasizing the main subject. This method can highlight the tree's intricate features, such as its delicate branching or textured bark.

Images that are distinctive and captivating can be made by experimenting with perspective. Photographers can convey a sense of scale, highlighting the miniature nature of bonsai, by juxtaposing the bonsai tree with components of its surroundings or using inventive angles. To give the image dimension and context, experiment with the foreground and background elements.

Written documentation is crucial for maintaining the background and specifics of each bonsai tree, in addition to images. It contains details regarding the tree's species, the styling methods employed, notable turning points, and any other noteworthy developments. A fuller comprehension of the tree's journey is made possible by the written descriptions, which offer a story to go along with the visual evidence.

Online communities and social media have developed into useful tools for sharing and interacting with the global bonsai community in the digital age. On specialized bonsai websites, forums, and social media channels, images and written documentation can be shared. By facilitating cooperation, feedback, and educational opportunities, these platforms enable bonsai enthusiasts to interact with one another and gain insightful and varied viewpoints.

The beauty, artistry, and history of bonsai trees must be captured and preserved through artistic bonsai photography and documentation. The artistry and individuality of each bonsai may be highlighted and shared with a wider audience through expert photography techniques and thorough documentation. Bonsai enthusiasts can encourage deeper appreciation for this ancient art form by fusing verbal and visual components. In addition to preserving the legacy of specific trees, artistic bonsai photography and documentation increase public understanding of and appreciation for bonsai as a living art form.

Bonsai as a lifelong journey: connecting with the bonsai community

Bonsai is a lifelong journey of learning, connection, and growth; it is not just a pastime or a simple collection of trees. The maintenance and styling of small trees is just one aspect of the bonsai art, which also includes the profound experiences and relationships developed within the bonsai community. In this section, we'll look at how bonsai may be a lifelong adventure and the value of networking with other bonsai enthusiasts to promote development, share knowledge, and create lasting relationships.

We learn the value of patience from bonsai. We gradually develop our ability to see, comprehend, and react to the requirements of the trees as we take care of and nurture these living works of art. As we investigate the nuances of horticulture, styling methods, and the beauty behind each tree, bonsai demands ongoing study. It is a path that promotes self-improvement, resiliency, and the formation of a great attention to detail.

Artistic expression and creativity are encouraged by bonsai. As we learn about different bonsai styles, aesthetics, and design concepts, we refine our sense of balance, proportion, and harmony. The path of bonsai enables us to develop our own distinct aesthetic and artistic vision, continuously expanding and honing our abilities as we engage with other trees and accept fresh viewpoints.

The bonsai community is an excellent source for learning and growth. Making connections with like-minded individuals, going to workshops, and taking part in exhibitions are opportunities to exchange information, techniques, and experiences. The community's combined knowledge deepens our grasp of bonsai and quickens our learning curve. We learn new things, solve problems, and broaden our horizons by exchanging experiences.

Bonsai encourages a spirit of teamwork and friendship. The passion of this ancient art form unites bonsai enthusiasts in a way that cuts through national borders and cultural barriers. Building enduring connections with people who share your interests through involvement in the bonsai community can help you create a network of friends, mentors, and fellow students as well as a support system.

Exhibitions of bonsai are colorful displays of skill and commitment. We can observe the skill and variety of bonsai by visiting exhibitions, which offers an immersive experience. These gatherings provide chances to interact with well-known artists, share thoughts, and find inspiration for our individual bonsai journeys. Exhibitions give us a chance to show off our original works while obtaining feedback and praise from others.

A bonsai club or organization membership has many advantages. These groups hold regular gatherings, workshops, and demonstrations where members can pick the brains of seasoned professionals and impart their own wisdom. The community's connections are strengthened through the frequent group events that bonsai clubs plan, such as collecting trips, study tours, and cooperative projects.

Online forums and social media sites have developed into effective tools for bringing together bonsai enthusiasts around the world in the digital era. These websites make it easier to share information, stories, and images about bonsai trees. A variety of opinions can be acquired through conversation in online forums, blogs, and social media groups. We may interact with bonsai enthusiasts who may be geographically separated but have the same enthusiasm due to virtual connections.

Online groups are a constant source of inspiration since bonsai enthusiasts share their works, methods, and progress reports. Through these forums, we may ask for help, work out problems, and get inspiration from other enthusiasts, which helps us stay committed to the lifelong bonsai adventure.

In conclusion, bonsai is more than just growing little trees; it's a lifelong journey. It provides a route for creative expression, personal development, and interaction with a thriving group of like-minded people. Engaging with the bonsai community offers chances to discover, impart knowledge, and create lasting relationships. Connecting with the bonsai community, whether through local clubs, exhibitions, internet resources, or social media, broadens our understanding of this ancient art form and increases our appreciation for it. Along this lifelong journey, we not only care for and shape the trees, but we also nurture our own personal development and the growth of the greater bonsai community.

CONCLUSION

Recap of key bonsai principles and techniques

Throughout the course of this e-book, we have delved into numerous areas of bonsai cultivation, design, care, and aesthetic expression as we have investigated the fascinating world of bonsai. As we approach the end of our journey, it is important to review the fundamental ideas and practices that form the basis of the art of bonsai. The purpose of this recap is to serve as a full review, with a focus on the essential ideas and procedures that are required for successful bonsai growth. Bonsai enthusiasts can reinforce their understanding, refine their skills, and continue their path toward producing living works of art by reviewing these principles and techniques.

A Comprehension of the Bonsai Principles

Proportion and Scale: Bonsai is the art of creating miniature trees that imitate the proportions and scale of full-sized trees seen in nature. This is accomplished by reducing the size of the tree while maintaining its natural form. The bonsai tree will appear harmonic and balanced only if the principles of proportion and scale are understood and used correctly.

Creating Balance and Harmony: Creating balance and harmony in a bonsai design requires careful consideration of the distribution of foliage, branches, and negative space within the design. The use of this principle results in a sense of equilibrium as well as aesthetic appeal.

Elegance and Simplicity: By eliminating extraneous components and emphasizing the tree's primary characteristics, bonsai emphasizes simplicity and elegance. By taking this method, the observer is given the opportunity to admire the inherent beauty and form of the tree.

Continuity and Flow: One of the primary goals of bonsai design is to produce a sense of continuity and flow by imitating the organic development patterns that may be found in nature. The transition from one branch to the next should be seamless, leading the observer's gaze along a route that is aesthetically pleasant.

Techniques for Bonsai Care and Cultivation

Pruning and Shaping: Pruning is a fundamental technique in the cultivation of bonsai, as it encourages growth, helps to maintain shape, and refines the tree's overall aesthetic. Regular pruning allows for more control over the size and direction of branch growth, as well as the promotion of back budding, which results in denser foliage.

Wiring and Styling: Wiring is used to shape and place branches, hence creating desired forms and silhouettes. Styling refers to the process of shaping and positioning the branches. The application of wire in a careful manner causes the least amount of damage possible to the tree while still enabling aesthetic customization.

Repotting and Root Pruning: Repotting is essential for preserving the health and vitality of bonsai. It is necessary to remove the tree from its container, do root trimming and pruning, and then replant the tree in fresh soil as part of this process. When done correctly, repotting ensures that there is sufficient drainage and creates space for new root growth.

Fertilization and Watering: For bonsai health, appropriate watering methods are essential. It is essential to provide the tree with the appropriate amount of moisture while avoiding either waterlogging or drying out the roots. In addition, the provision of adequate fertilization provides the vital nutrients that are required for healthy growth.

Bonsai Design Styles

Formal Upright Style: The formal upright style is a representation of the traditional shape of a tree, which is characterized by a straight, upright trunk and branches that gradually taper outward. It gives off the impression of sturdiness and elegance all at the same time.

Informal Upright Style: The informal upright style is characterized by a trunk that is curved or slightly slanted, resembling a tree that has grown in its natural environment over time. It lends the appearance of ease and naturalism to the overall presentation.

Cascade Style: The cascade style features a trunk that cascades downward, often resembling the image of a tree that is growing on a cliff or at the edge of the water. It gives off the impression of excitement, movement, and dynamic energy.

Windswept Style: A tree in the windswept style has branches and the trunk bent and twisted in a particular direction, giving the impression that it has withstood strong winds. It gives off the impression of resiliency and adaptability.

Bonsai Display and Presentation

Choosing the Right Pot: A suitable pot complements the tree's style and improves its overall presentation. Aspects such as color, shape, and material must be chosen that are compatible with the aesthetics of the tree.

Considerations for Display: When displaying a bonsai tree, it is important to take into account various elements, including background color, lighting, and how the tree will look in relation to other plants and objects. The natural beauty of the bonsai can be brought out to its full potential by establishing a setting that is aesthetically pleasing.

Seasonal Considerations: Seasonal elements like winter decorations, flowering plants, or autumn foliage can improve bonsai displays. These additions provide for a dynamic show that is constantly evolving throughout the course of the year.

Continued Learning and Evolution

Study and observation: Growing a bonsai requires ongoing education. Continuous study, observation, and enjoyment of bonsai as well as nature are all helpful in refining skills and developing a deeper grasp on both subjects.

Participating in the Bonsai: Community Interacting with other people who share an interest in bonsai, going to workshops and exhibitions, and becoming a member of a bonsai club all provide opportunities to learn, exchange information, and find new sources of motivation.

Experimentation and Creativity: Bonsai encourages both artistic expression and experimentation. As a bonsai artist, cultivating your creativity and developing yourself as a person both benefit from trying out various methods, styles, and techniques.

In conclusion, the art of bonsai is comprised of a vast tapestry of different concepts and methods, and it exemplifies a harmonious equilibrium between the creative potential of humans and the natural world. Enthusiasts can make attractive miniature trees if they are familiar with and use the principles of proportion, balance, simplicity, and continuity. Bonsai enthusiasts are able to better shape their trees and provide proper care for them once they have mastered several procedures, such as wiring, repotting, and pruning. Bonsai enthusiasts can better exhibit the beauty of their works if they have a solid understanding of the many bonsai styles and display concerns. In addition, the path of bonsai is a lifelong quest of learning, developing, and engaging with the greater community of bonsai practitioners. Bonsai enthusiasts will find fulfillment in their continued bonsai adventure as they continue to hone their skills and learn more about the ancient art form of bonsai, with all of its limitless potential applications.

Encouragement and inspiration for beginners

Beginning the path of cultivating bonsai may be both exhilarating and daunting for those who are just starting out with this journey. It is a form of art that demands patience, dedication, and a willingness to learn, but it is also very captivating. In this section, we will discuss the significance of providing novices with support and inspiration as they embark on their bonsai journey. We will go through strategies for overcoming obstacles, finding sources of encouragement, and locating mentors so that you can develop a successful bonsai practice. Beginners can experience success in their pursuit of this traditional art form if they are provided with a nurturing environment and access to relevant resources.

Realistic Expectations: It's important for newcomers to realize that bonsai requires a commitment over an extended period of time. The process of growth and development takes time, and trees progress gradually over their lifetimes. By having reasonable expectations, beginners can avoid being frustrated and learn to appreciate the gradual but ultimately satisfying development of their bonsai trees.

Accepting Mistakes: A crucial aspect of the bonsai journey is learning from mistakes. Inexperienced individuals should not let failures discourage them but rather see them as opportunities to learn useful lessons. Every setback presents an opportunity to improve one's strategies, acquire more information, and strengthen one's willpower.

Celebrating Minor Wins: Bonsai is a lifelong process of learning and development. Beginners should make a point of commemorating each significant achievement, whether they have successfully wired a branch, achieved healthy growth, or created an attractive design. Beginners are encouraged to maintain their motivation and inspiration when their progress is acknowledged.

Studying Bonsai Masters: Bonsai masters' knowledge and experiences are a tremendous source of inspiration. Investigating their body of work, reading their books, and participating in their demonstrations or workshops can result in the acquisition of insightful knowledge and the rekindling of an interest in the art form.

Exploring Bonsai Gardens and Exhibits: Going to bonsai gardens and exhibits gives you the opportunity to view breathtaking bonsai collections and observe the artistry of highly talented practitioners. The intricate designs and varied aesthetics of bonsai trees can be a great source of inspiration for those just starting out in the art.

Getting Involved with the Bonsai Community: For beginners, joining clubs or online communities, talking to other enthusiasts, and taking part in bonsai workshops can help build a strong support system. A sense of community and inspiration can be fostered by the exchange of experiences, the seeking of assistance, and the attendance at events relevant to bonsai.

Finding a Mentor: For newcomers, a mentor is quite helpful. A mentor is someone who can provide assistance, share their skills, and give personalized input on procedures and the maintenance of trees. Creating a relationship between a mentor and a mentee offers a supportive setting that is conducive to personal growth and development.

Attending Workshops and Courses: Attending bonsai workshops and courses provides beginners with the opportunity to learn from more experienced instructors, gain experience working with their hands, and develop more practical abilities. These organized classroom settings offer concentrated instruction that is catered to the specific requirements of first-timers.

Making Use of Online Resources: For those who are interested in bonsai, the internet is a wealth of knowledge and resources. Tutorials, forums, and instructional videos are all available online for beginners to use in order to learn methods, resolve problems, and look for inspiration.

Patience and Perseverance: Bonsai is a patient art that calls for perseverance and dedication. It is crucial for novices to acquire patience and accept the process, understanding that each stage of development contributes to the masterpiece that will ultimately be created.

Adapting to New Situations: Bonsai trees are living things that alter in response to their surroundings. Those who are just starting out need to understand how to modify their care and practices appropriately, taking into account elements such as climate, seasonality, and the tree's overall health.

Dealing with Obstacles: Just like any other living thing, bonsai trees may experience obstacles like pests, illnesses, or environmental stress. In order to maintain the health and vitality of their trees, beginners should arm themselves with the knowledge necessary to properly detect and quickly treat any problems that may arise.

Technique Exploration: The art of bonsai allows you a lot of room for creative expression and personal growth. Experimenting with different strategies, such as various styles of pruning, wiring methods, and design approaches, is recommended for beginners. They will be able to uncover their preferences and craft their own unique style as a result of this experimentation.

Connecting with the Tree's Story: Every bonsai tree has a distinct past and personality. Finding a connection with the tree's history, learning about its species, and admiring the tree for its unique beauty are all great places for beginners to look for inspiration. The experience of bonsai is elevated as a result of this connection, and the artistic expression is given greater depth as a result.

Documenting the journey: Keeping a record of bonsai development in the form of images, written observations, or a bonsai diary offers a concrete means to monitor development and consider the journey as a whole. Beginners are able to reflect on their accomplishments and gain wisdom from their experiences by means of documentation.

In conclusion, encouragement and inspiration are vital components in the process of cultivating the bonsai journey for novices. Beginners can overcome obstacles and cultivate their passion for bonsai by embracing the process of learning, finding inspiration from masters and bonsai exhibits, and seeking help from mentors and instructional materials. Important characteristics to hone include tenacity, patience, and the capacity to re-adjust one's behavior in response to shifting conditions. The experience of bonsai can be made richer and more satisfying through the development of a personal style and through establishing a connection with the story of the tree. Beginners can embark on a meaningful journey of artistic expression and personal growth in the world of bonsai if they have an environment that is supportive of their endeavors and a mindset that is focused on constant learning.

Final thoughts on the art and science of growing miniature trees

As we approach the end of our journey into the art and science of cultivating miniature trees, it is essential to pause and contemplate the tremendous beauty and transformational power of bonsai. We have looked into a variety of aspects of bonsai cultivation throughout the course of this e-book, including its history, techniques, principles, as well as the challenges and rewards associated with it. In this final section, we will discuss some concluding ideas regarding the art and science of bonsai, as well as provide a summary of the most important takeaways from our journey.

The Harmony of Art and Science

Bonsai is an extraordinary form of miniature cultivation that combines artistic skill with scientific understanding. It blends an in-depth grasp of horticulture and tree biology with aesthetic ideals such as proportion, balance, and harmony. The design and styling of the tree are where the creativity comes into play, while the science behind it is what insures its health, development, and longevity. In order to create pieces of living art, bonsai cultivators need to have a firm grasp of both elements.

The Strength of Time and Patience

The art form known as bonsai acknowledges and celebrates the passage of time through its practice. The growth and development of a bonsai tree occur gradually over time, with patience, keen observation, and careful attention to detail. The bonsai tree, over the course of its cultivation, transforms into a representation of the cultivator's commitment, tenacity, and reverence for the natural world as it matures. The art of bonsai teaches us the importance of having patience as well as the beauty that can be discovered in the passing of time.

The Role of Nature and Collaboration

The art of bonsai is the result of a collaboration between human ingenuity and the innate allure of the natural world. The growth of the tree is directed by the cultivator through the use of methods like as pruning, wiring, and shaping. This is done in cooperation with the natural processes that occur. However, they are also required to acknowledge the bounds of their control and acknowledge the role that nature plays in determining the final outcome. The art of bonsai instills in us a sense of humility and serves as a constant reminder that we are merely custodians of the natural environment.

The Never-Ending Quest for Knowledge and Personal Development

The art form known as bonsai presents its practitioners with countless opportunities for personal development and intellectual expansion. It is a path that lasts a lifetime and enables cultivators to consistently hone their abilities, delve deeper into their knowledge, and investigate fresh opportunities for creative expression. Bonsai is not just about making beautiful trees, but also about personal growth, self-expression, and establishing a relationship with the natural world. It inspires us to remain learners for the rest of our lives and to welcome the challenges and satisfactions that come with consistent development.

The Connection to Tradition and Culture

The art of bonsai is deeply rooted in tradition and has its origins in a culturally significant past. It has been handed down from generation to generation since it was first practiced in ancient China and Japan. The development of bonsai provides a connection to this cultural past and paves the way for an appreciation of the art form's inherent knowledge, craftsmanship, and spiritual value. This appreciation can be gained by participation in bonsai activities. The art of bonsai connects us to the practices of our ancestors and serves as a connection between the past and the present.

The Benefits and Satisfaction that come with Bonsai

The practice of bonsai can result in a variety of benefits. A sense of responsibility, nurturing, and care can be developed through the process of bonsai tree cultivation. A profound sense of satisfaction and fulfillment is brought about by experiencing the joy of seeing the tree flourish due to our care for it. Additionally, bonsai offers opportunities for stillness, introspection, and reconnection with the natural world. It teaches us to discover harmony within ourselves and with the world around us, as well as to appreciate the beauty that can be found in the smallest of things.

In conclusion, the practice of bonsai, which refers to the art and science of cultivating miniature trees, is an activity that is both intriguing and transformational. It requires artistic talent, scientific knowledge, patient observation, and cooperative effort with natural elements. Bonsai growers go on a never-ending quest for knowledge and development, forging connections with history, culture, and the innate splendor of the natural world.

It is essential, as we get to the end of this e-book, to recognize that bonsai is more than just the nurturing of miniature trees; rather, it is a way of life. It teaches us priceless lessons about the value of observation, patience, and resiliency in the face of adversity. The art of bonsai urges us to accept the passing of time, recognize the value of the flawed beauty that exists all around us, and seek solace in the natural world.

There is no limit to the amount of self-expression, creative potential, and personal fulfillment that may be achieved through bonsai, regardless of your level of experience as a cultivator. Therefore, let us continue to cultivate the art and science of bonsai, valuing each tree that we cultivate and the insight that it provides to us. I hope that our journey into the world of bonsai will be one that is rich in aesthetic experience, personal development, and a profound connection to the magnificent world of tree-like miniatures.

Thank you for buying and reading/listening to our book.
If you found this book useful/helpful please take a few minutes
and leave a review on Amazon.com or Audible.com
(if you bought the audio version).